P9-BHY-586

STUDY SKILLS

Do I really need this stuff?

Steve Piscitelli

FLORIDA COMMUNITY COLLEGE AT JACKSONVILLE

CAUTION: READ THESE MODULES ONLY IF YOU HAVE THE DESIRE TO IMPROVE YOUR SCHOOL PERFORMANCE

PEARSON

Prentice
Hall

Upper Saddle River, New Jersey
Columbus, Ohio

Library of Congress Cataloging-in-Publication Data

Piscitelli, Stephen.
    Study skills : do I really need this stuff? / Steve Piscitelli.
        p.   cm.
    Includes bibliographical references (p. 215) and index.
        ISBN 0-13-112340-8
        1. Study skills.   2. College student orientation.   I. Title.

LB2395 .P59 2004
378.1'70281—dc21

                                        2003045614

Vice President and Publisher: Jeffery W. Johnston
Senior Acquisitions Editor: Sande Johnson
Assistant Editor: Cecilia Johnson
Editorial Assistant: Erin Anderson
Production Editor: Holcomb Hathaway
Design Coordinator: Diane C. Lorenzo
Cover Designer: Ali Mohrman
Cover Photo: Getty One
Production Manager: Pamela D. Bennett
Director of Marketing: Ann Castel Davis
Director of Advertising: Kevin Flanagan
Marketing Manager: Christina Quadhamer
Compositor: Aerocraft Charter Art Service
Cover Printer: Phoenix Color Corp.
Printer/Binder: Courier Kendallville, Inc.

DEDICATION

*To Tom Hopper,
a man of quiet integrity.*

Copyright © 2004 by Pearson Education, Inc., Upper Saddle River, New Jersey, 07458.
Pearson Prentice Hall. All rights reserved. Printed in the United States of America. This publication is protected by
Copyright and permission should be obtained from the publisher prior to any prohibited reproduction, storage in a
retrieval system, or transmission in any form or by any means, electronic, mechanical, photocopying, recording, or
likewise. For information regarding permission(s), write to: Rights and Permissions Department.

Pearson Prentice Hall™ is a trademark of Pearson Education, Inc.
Pearson® is a registered trademark of Pearson plc
Prentice Hall® is a registered trademark of Pearson Education, Inc.

Pearson Education Ltd.
Pearson Education Australia Pty. Limited
Pearson Education Singapore Pte. Ltd.
Pearson Education North Asia Ltd.
Pearson Education Canada, Ltd.
Pearson Educación de Mexico, S.A. de C.V.
Pearson Education–Japan
Pearson Education Malaysia Pte. Ltd.

10 9 8 7 6 5 4 3 2
ISBN 0-13-112340-8

BRIEF CONTENTS

CONTENTS

MODULE 5

5 *The Classroom Experience* 93

ACHIEVING THE BEST RESULT

MODULE 8 *Memory*   175

WHATSHISNAME SCHEDULED A WHATCHAMACALLIT FOR WHEN?

MODULE 9 *Test Preparation*   195

THERE'S NO BUSINESS LIKE PREP BUSINESS

PREFACE

Study Skills: Do I Really Need This Stuff? is a student-friendly volume of practical study strategies and tips for immediate application in classroom situations. The numerous reflective activities are designed to help students become more aware of their strengths and challenges. This book also demonstrates how *academic* study skills readily relate to the *world of work*.

Students lead busy lives. Too often, they are left wondering what the connection is between the classroom and the real world. This book bridges that gap.

FEATURES OF THIS BOOK

- The SAC-SIP[1] problem-solving model is used throughout the modules.

- A section on multiple intelligences is provided in Module 2.

- A section on handling criticism is included.

- Guidelines for evaluating Internet sites give students tips for determining the credibility and validity of sites.

- Workforce case studies show students how to apply study skill strategies in a workplace environment.

- Tips and strategies are clearly labeled throughout the modules as "success strategies," accompanied by the icon you see in the margin.

- Module overviews show how the particular module fits into the overall structure of the book. Specific module headings are also featured.

- More than 30 reflective activities, along with 6 workplace case studies, complement the strategies.

- Forty-five exhibits enhance the concepts with visual explanations.

- End-of-module data retrieval charts help to organize main points and correlate with learning styles and multiple intelligences.

- End-of-module questions provide a quick check on key points.

- Footnotes provide students with readily accessible additional information.

- A bibliography of selected resources provides direction to complementary source material.

- An index allows specific information to be easily located.

SUCCESS STRATEGY

---

[1]This acronym is explained fully in Module 1. The letters stand for *stop, alternatives, consequences, select, implement,* and *pause.*

THE STRUCTURE OF THIS BOOK

Although organization is the basis for all study skills, not every student needs to devote equal time to each skill. "So," I asked myself, "why make a student wade through an entire book? Why not break the material into more bite-sized and meaningful parts?"

The result you have in your hands. This layout is designed to help you become a more efficient and effective student. A brief overview of the modules follows. You may reorder (but *never* ignore!) the information in a way that best serves your needs.

Module 1: Identifying and meeting your challenges

- It comes down to a couple of principles. The P.O.P. R.A.P.[2] list summarizes the main principles of the modules. These strategies work in the classroom and will have practical application in everyday life—honestly! Review the strategies in these modules. Select according to your personality and what works for you. These strategies have helped students minimize failures and maximize successes. They can help you, too.

- Discussion focuses on the top 10 challenges all students face, as well as the characteristics of successful students.

- A strategy to handle criticism effectively is introduced. A workforce case study allows you to apply newly learned skills.

- The SAC-SIP problem-solving model is introduced. A workforce case study provides the opportunity for you to apply newly learned skills.

- A "Covenant with Myself" asks for a personal commitment to student success.

Module 2: Learning styles and multiple intelligences

- The concept of learning styles is introduced. An informal learning style assessment is presented. This information sets the foundation for the rest of the book. Each succeeding module ends with suggested ways to correlate learning style to some of the strategies presented in the preceding pages.

- An overview of multiple intelligences presents more strategies for success. Each succeeding module will match selected intelligences to module topics.

Module 3: Goal setting

- You will be guided through the process of establishing meaningful and realistic goals. Activities include an analysis of study skill scenarios and an assessment of strengths and weaknesses. These activities concentrate on the need to have focused direction in academics *and* life in general.

- A systematic model helps you establish long-range, midrange, and short-range goals.

---

[2]This acronym stands for six basic principles of study skills: know your *purpose*, *organize* material, remain *positive*, *review* regularly, engage in *active* learning, and *pick* the methods that work for you.

Module 4: Time management

- This module naturally transitions from the last one. Now that a goal has given you a purpose, it is time to organize for action and get out of your own way. The module activities allow for more self-assessment: What causes time-management problems? How do you spend a typical 168-hour week? What seem to be the major time-wasters in your life? Other activities show you how to break down far-off deadlines and larger-than-life projects into simpler, more manageable, bite-sized steps. A workforce case study allows you to apply newly learned skills.

- Time management is a matter of priorities. This is more than a "let's-put-it-on-a-calendar" section; you will not only learn the art of prioritizing tasks, but also how to maintain a balance in academic life. "Urgency," "importance," "effectiveness," and "efficiency" are placed in a realistic context for you.

Module 5: The classroom experience

- What is that teacher doing in front of the classroom? Like it or not, each instructor has a unique style of delivery and a particular emphasis in class. The successful student understands these styles and works with them. Common classroom distractions are presented along with strategies to combat them.

- What are you doing in the back of the classroom? The teacher has a job—and so does the student. This section starts with a quick review of how a student can influence the mood of the classroom. Active learning, note-taking strategies, and effective review techniques (the 3Rs and TSDs[3]) provide a basis for success. As with other topics, organization is vital. You will be able to practice various strategies to organize and reorganize material so that you can understand the big picture as well as the supporting details.

Module 6: Reading with a purpose

- To understand a reading assignment, the student must first approach it in an organized fashion. Reading an assignment "because the instructor told me to" is *not* a purpose. Rare is the student who finds the class text interesting. An effective reading plan will allow you to navigate successfully the vagaries of a reading assignment.

- Strategies are also provided for reading novels and keeping pace with the instructor's class lectures.

Module 7: Basic writing tips

- This module provides a simple approach to get you started and focused—even in the face of writing blocks—until the final product is ready for teacher review. The T.O.E.S. (topic, opinion, evidence, and summary) method of organization provides a simple writing formula. A

---

[3]The 3Rs stands for review, relate, and reorganize; TSDs stands for title, summary, and details.

10-point writing checklist creates a quick, yet effective tool to self-evaluate a paper before turning it in. A workforce case study allows you to apply newly learned skills.

■ Once you get over the initial shock of having to prepare a major research paper, you will need to know where to start and how to proceed. A general overview of the nuts and bolts of narrowing a topic, managing time, and negotiating the library is presented. Evaluation guidelines will help you to determine the credibility of Internet sites.

Module 8: Memory

■ Why do we forget? A key to a more effective memory is concentration. Causes for retrieval failure, as well as strategies to improve retention and recall, are discussed in this module. Memory is a matter of focusing energies. Active listening, data retrieval chart development, peg systems, acronyms, and acrostics are some of the techniques introduced to foster retention and retrieval.

■ The activities reinforce the need to establish relationships—which ties in with strategies introduced in previous topics. A workforce case study allows you to apply newly learned skills.

Module 9: Test preparation

■ Just what is test anxiety and how can a student overcome it? Is test anxiety the problem, or is it test-taking inefficiency? The strategies in this module not only build on the previous modules, but also set the stage for more goal setting—which brings us back to the first module.

■ A test-preparation checklist not only guides you through the "get-ready" phase of studying for a test, but emphasizes the importance of a post-exam analysis. Tips help with "emergency studying"—that is, cramming. A workforce case study allows you to apply newly learned skills.

ACKNOWLEDGMENTS

I would like to thank former student Terry Kauppila for taking the time to review and comment on the case studies; Warren Grymes for sharing ideas on the connection between the classroom and the workplace; Cheryl Grymes for reminding me that we can make a difference one step at a time; Mary Hamra for her initial support of the project; Victoria McGlone for her capable research guidance; and Carolyn Phanstiel for exemplifying the meaning of *mentor*. As always, I continue to learn from my students and colleagues. Special thanks to my editor, Sande Johnson. Her calm and focused direction has been invaluable. Cecilia Johnson helped me through much of the process of the publishing industry with step-by-step advice that put all the pieces in an understandable order.

My sincere thanks go to the reviewers of this text, who offered constructive suggestions for its improvement. They are:

Christina Chapman, Lewis and Clark Community College

Valerie DeAngelis, Miami Dade Community College

Angela Gibson, South Texas Community College

Lewis Gray, Middle Tennessee State

Katherine Mills, Anne Arundle Community College

Jeanie Nishime, Pasadena City College

Laura L. Reynolds, Clover Park Technical College

Anita Smith, Columbia Basin College

Special thanks go to my wife, Laurie, for once again sharing her time as I worked on this project. A model of patience, she is a continuing inspiration.

ABOUT THE AUTHOR

Steve Piscitelli has more than two decades of teaching experience. He has taught students of varying abilities and grade levels, from seventh grade to the college level. He has been recognized for his effective teaching style with awards at the school, county, and international level. In 2002, Steve received the Florida Community College at Jacksonville Outstanding Faculty Award for innovation in teaching. He is currently a professor of history and education at Florida Community College at Jacksonville.

Steve received an undergraduate degree from Jacksonville University, an M.Ed. from the University of North Florida, and an M.A. (United States history) from the University of Florida.

In addition to this book, he is the author of numerous articles and a history review book for students.

Steve lives with his wife, Laurie, in Atlantic Beach, Florida.

IDENTIFYING AND MEETING YOUR CHALLENGES

Organizing for success

"The future belongs to those who believe in their dreams."

—ELEANOR ROOSEVELT,

FIRST LADY OF THE UNITED STATES FROM 1933 TO 1945

MODULE 1

Overview of This Module

WHAT ARE THESE MODULES ALL ABOUT ANYWAY?

WHAT ARE STUDY SKILLS, AND WHY DO I NEED THEM?

A QUICK REVIEW

WHAT ARE THESE MODULES ALL ABOUT ANYWAY?

Effective study and organizational skills come down to a few major principles. Each author and instructor has a different approach—but the bottom line is the same.

As you use these modules, you will quickly notice that this is not rocket science. There is a reason, when I speak to teachers, students, and parents, that the title of my workshop generally is "The Not-So-Secret Secrets of Student Success."

Helpful sources flood the market today that address the topics these modules do. I have listed some of these works in the bibliography. I believe, however, that these modules go further. For instance:

- The topic is serious but the tone is light. You will not get lost in research jargon or confusing graphics.

- The techniques have been developed, refined, and used in classrooms and seminars.

---

[1]Here I am applying the "acronym" strategy introduced in Module 8.

- The material is fresh. College students are currently using these tips.
- The strategies are applicable to the classroom as well as the workplace.

As you read the strategies and tips in this and the other eight modules, you will probably say to yourself, "That's obvious. I already know that!" And, you are probably right. There are no secrets here. These strategies will help you focus the energies you already have. The modules, as a whole, should help you add to your bag of academic tools so that you may conquer any academic challenge.

The P.O.P. R.A.P. list

If you take nothing else from each of the modules, remember these basic principles:

- **P: Know your *purpose* and mission as a student.** You have to make the commitment to focus on success and be a successful student.
- **O: *Organize* your time.** To be a successful student you must take charge of your time. You cannot control others—but you sure can control your own actions.
- **P: Be *positive*.** Don't hinder yourself with defeatist attitudes. Visualize success and shoot for it. Be realistic but also challenge yourself.
- **R: *Review*, reorganize, and relate.** There is a difference between memorizing and understanding. You will be exposed to a great deal of material in college. Get in the habit of finding connections among your assigned readings, class notes, and discussions. Once you learn how to do this, you will have a better command of the material before you.
- **A: Be an *active* learner.** Know where your instructors are going with a lesson. Don't just sit there. Follow them—maybe even get there ahead of them.
- **P: *Pick* and mix and match these strategies to suit your personality and learning style.** Adapt these strategies to your learning style, practice them faithfully, and apply them to your studies. You will see improvement. Studying is a process. It is *not* a "get rich" scheme for you to gain good grades with little effort.

Is there a common thread to these modules?

You had better believe there is a commonality!

The core structure of study skills is *critical thinking*. Critical thinkers are active learners who do not stop asking questions about whatever is before them. They are problem solvers. With practice, you will learn to ask focused questions. This will foster an organized approach to problem solving, which will help you see patterns and monitor your thinking process.

No matter what module or modules you choose to tackle, you will see a common emphasis on problem solving. This may be stated overtly or quietly lying beneath the surface, so be assured that the process is always there. Also, know that the problem-solving model introduced in this module works in the classroom *and* the workplace. Other strategies also go beyond the classroom. For instance, case studies will help you make the connection from the classroom to the workplace. Learn the strategies and apply them as often as possible. Have confidence in your ability to do well.

Finally, before we start, keep in mind that the strategies found in these modules are virtually useless unless you take the time to practice them, study them, and apply them. When you find a reflective self-assessment activity in a module, set aside some quiet time for yourself and complete it carefully. After all, the time you invest in these modules is time you are investing in yourself. I can think of no better investment. Can you?

What will *not* happen by using this material?

Some books offer ways to "beat the system" in order for students to earn the highest possible grade. That is like going on a trendy diet to lose weight but never changing the behaviors that resulted in the undesired extra baggage. If it were as simple as just reading a book or watching a video, you, your class-mates, and most other students would be happy with high GPAs. Unfortunately, it's not that easy. So if you want a quick-fix approach offering instant gratification, these modules are not for you. Of course, there is noth-ing wrong with going for the best grade, but you need to focus on your behaviors. These modules will help you do just that! However, you have to be diligent and accept responsibility along the way.

What *will* happen by using this material?

This material will help you identify and change those behaviors that are keep-ing you from being the very best student you can be. Its overriding purpose is to help you focus on your strengths while working to reduce your weakness-es. The central concept is organization. Good study habits do not necessarily mean an increased workload, but efficient studying allows you to study more effectively.

These modules concentrate on practical skills to build academic success as well as a positive self-image. While these strategies are worthwhile for students at every level, they are particularly valuable to those individuals who have the *potential and desire,* in an increasingly competitive academic world, to obtain the "added edge" needed for academic success.

These skills help you make the transition from being a student who simply gets by, to being a successful student who is shrewd, insightful, and confident.

To achieve at above-average academic levels, *you* need to develop tech-niques to *focus* your energies on efficient and effective studying. Additionally, effectively applied study skills are crucial in the development of *positive self-esteem.* A student who can achieve in the classroom will feel better about his or her capabilities. In other words, *competence will foster esteem.*

Specifically, if you diligently follow the suggestions in these modules you will learn the following:

- The tips and strategies I provide will help you become a more effective and efficient student. Once I present these techniques, my job is com-plete—and yours is really just beginning. You will need to commit to three tasks: *learn* the strategies, *use* the strategies immediately, and con-tinually *practice* the strategies.

- One size does not fit all. Each of us has a unique learning style. Identify it; make adjustments and see the success.

- The motivation to do well is really within you. External influences may cause a temporary burst of inspiration. For the long term, however, you must have confidence in your abilities, address your shortcomings, and develop skills that will guide you through school—and through life.

- All of the strategies come down to organization. The successful students have it; those without it struggle.

- The strategies are also excellent life-management tools. These techniques are *easily transferable to everyday life and the workplace.*

This book is the result of ongoing experience with students. These techniques work. Learn them, practice them, and apply them. **You *can* become a successful student.**

Top 10 challenges all students must face

Each grade in school, each level in a vocational program, and each year in college has its own set of challenges. Regardless of the year of education or the age of the student, there are certain challenges with which all students must grapple. The following modules will deal with each. Most will overlap as we move through the activities, tips, and strategies.

For the moment, though, let's see how you measure up in regard to the challenges discussed in Activity 1.1. For each of the questions in Activity 1.1, take a moment and jot down some honest answers. Use extra paper as needed. Remember, if you are less than truthful, you might as well skip the activity. Don't waste your time if you are not serious about improving.

I really do want to learn—but I just can't!

It is frustrating to have the desire to learn but come up short on result. As you complete the following assessment, identify obstacles to your learning as well as the strengths that help you learn. What stands in your way of being as successful as you would like? Are these obstacles related to attitude or ability? What strengths have helped you in the past to achieve in the classroom?

Let's look at Activity 1.2, "Assessment of Strengths and Weaknesses." What are some of your academic challenges?

As you completed Activity 1.2, did you see any patterns developing in your responses? For instance, do you notice that you lack a focused plan of attack in most areas? Or do you see that you are strong in some areas, and weak in others?

Now go back to your notes in Activity 1.1 and rank order each item from 1 to 10. That is, place a *1* beside the item that represents your biggest challenge, followed by a *2* for the next biggest and so on. Make one last review of the material, and then set it aside for now. You will come back to these notes in the next module when you examine how to set goals.

ACTIVITY 1.1   THE TOP 10 CHALLENGES

Use the following questions as motivators to start you thinking about these challenges. You do not need to answer each question.

ATTITUDE. Do you, more days than not, come to class with the correct frame of mind? That is, are you ready to learn? Are you enthusiastic? Are you cooperative with the teacher?

_____

_____

CONTROL. When you encounter a problem, do you know how to determine where the problem really lies? Do you know how to determine when and where you have the control to make a change? Do you know when the power to change is not in your hands?

_____

_____

CHANGE. How do you react when you find your old skills don't easily adapt to new situations? Do you throw up your hands and quit? What do you do when you come across a new teacher who is "hard"? How do you handle the class in which you will earn a lower grade than you are used to? Do you take control and look for a positive solution or do you look for a way to withdraw?

_____

_____

"I DON'TS!" This is my term to symbolize those continual problem areas that bother you. These are the areas in which you say, "I don't seem to be able to . . ." What are your "I don'ts"?

_____

_____

CHARTING A COURSE. Do you know in what direction you are heading as a student? Do you know what steps to take in order to reach your goals? Do your goals match what you think (at this point) is your life's mission?

_____

_____

PROCRASTINATION. Do you put things off when you could easily take care of them now? If you do, why do you do this? Are you even thinking of putting *this* activity off to another day?

_____

_____

_____

CLASSROOM SUCCESS. How are your classes alike? How do they differ? What do your teachers require?

_____

_____

_____

MEMORY. Do you often say, "I have a bad memory"? If yes, what is "bad" about your memory? What have you done to improve your memory?

_____

_____

_____

_____

READING WITH A PURPOSE. How do you attack a reading assignment? Do you just start? Do you know what to look for when you read? Or do you treat all words, all sections as equals?

_____

_____

_____

_____

EFFICIENT AND EFFECTIVE TEST-TAKING PROCEDURES. Are you anxious when it comes to taking tests? How do you prepare? Do you wait until the night before, or do you prepare each night? Do you know *how* to prepare on a nightly basis for a test that is two weeks away?

_____

_____

_____

_____

ACTIVITY 1.2 ASSESSMENT OF STRENGTHS AND WEAKNESSES

Before you can work on your challenges, you need to know what they are. That may seem obvious, but sometimes we miss the obvious. So, take a moment and complete the following checklist.

The challenges you want to concern yourself with at this point are *process* challenges, not *content* challenges. You might be weak solving mathematical equations, but concentrate on the *ways* in which you can become a more capable math student (or English, or history, or science, or Spanish, or some other class).

Check your **STRENGTHS** when it comes to studying. What do you do well? Check as many or as few as apply. Take your time and think about each choice carefully.

○ Setting goals

○ Completing goals

○ Establishing priorities

○ Completing work on time

○ Eliminating distractions

○ Taking notes from class lectures

○ Taking notes from the textbook

○ Taking organized notes

○ Getting to class on time

○ Participating in class

○ Keeping an organized notebook

○ Regularly reviewing class notes

○ Coming to class prepared

○ Getting the main point from a reading assignment

○ Writing a strong thesis statement

○ Being able to support an opinion with facts

○ Organizing an essay

○ Writing and completing an essay

○ Establishing relationships

○ Remembering important information for exams

○ Controlling test anxiety

○ Preparing, in plenty of time, for exams

○ Completing exams in the time allotted

○ Learning from previous exam mistakes

○ Taking study breaks

○ Studying alone

○ Studying with friends

○ Other: _____

Check your **WEAKNESSES** when it comes to studying. What do you need to improve? Check as many or as few as apply. Take your time and think about each choice carefully.

○ Setting goals

○ Completing goals

○ Establishing priorities

○ Completing work on time

○ Eliminating distractions

○ Taking notes from class lectures

○ Writing a strong thesis statement

○ Being able to support an opinion with facts

○ Organizing an essay

○ Writing and completing an essay

○ Establishing relationships

○ Remembering important information for exams

ASSESSMENT OF STRENGTHS AND WEAKNESSES, continued ACTIVITY 1.2

○ Taking notes from the textbook

○ Taking organized notes

○ Getting to class on time

○ Participating in class

○ Keeping an organized notebook

○ Regularly reviewing class notes

○ Getting the main point from a reading assignment

○ Coming to class prepared

○ Controlling test anxiety

○ Preparing, in plenty of time, for exams

○ Completing exams in the time allotted

○ Learning from previous exam mistakes

○ Taking study breaks

○ Studying alone

○ Studying with friends

○ Other: _____

_____

Rank order the top five items you checked in each section above. List below the five **strengths** you consider your biggest assets, ranking them from 1 to 5. Do the same for your **weaknesses**.

STRENGTHS

1. _____

2. _____

3. _____

4. _____

5. _____

WEAKNESSES

1. _____

2. _____

3. _____

4. _____

5. _____

All of the modules *concentrate on student behavior.* This is not to say that theory is unimportant. Educational theory underscores many of the concepts presented in the following pages. Sometimes, however, educational books are bogged down in dense jargon.

I have written these modules visualizing you, the student, sitting across the table from me, discussing and using the material presented. (That is one reason I make free use of the pronoun *you* throughout the modules.) It does not attempt to be all things to all students. The numerous informal, reflective self-assessment tools will help you connect, on an individual basis, with the process of becoming a more successful student. Moreover, these skills have value outside the classroom.

Problem solving for school and the workforce

The Internet is everywhere. Today we hear a lot about the World Wide Web (www). But there is another "www" with which we need to concern ourselves.

Too often, what we learn in school does not seem to have a direct connection to the *real* "www" of life: the *"wonderful world of work."* Study skills, if looked at in a broad sense, are really life skills. The modules here will emphasize these connections.

The common thread of *critical thinking* will be reinforced in this book with activities requiring you to rely on your *problem-solving skills.* There are various problem-solving models. All involve choice of one kind or another. Following is a two-tiered model: broad choice and specific choice. Pay close attention because you will be requested to revisit these models throughout the following modules.

SUCCESS STRATEGY

Broad choices: Adapting old skills to new situations

You are continually confronted with situations in which you must apply the skills you have developed over the years. You learn something in one school year or subject area (for example, how to take notes) and you must apply it in another school year or subject area. Occasionally, a new situation presents itself in which the old skills do not easily work. You must then make some sort of adjustment. In some cases, this may be minor; in others, quite dramatic. Frustration may very likely occur.

You have four broad choices:

1. **Quit** or remove yourself from the situation:
   - The new teacher is requiring things that you have either not done before or tried and not done well. Rather than confront the situation, you drop the class.
   - A similar scenario may be a catalyst for you to quit a job.
2. **Stay** in the new situation without adjusting your skills and suffer a miserable existence.
   - This situation is the same as the first except you cannot drop the class. You dislike the class, but you refuse to modify your skills. Consequently, you are one unhappy camper!

- Do you know someone who cannot adapt to a new boss or manager? Rather than looking for ways to improve the situation, the person suffers a miserable existence in the job.

3. **Modify** your skills to get by in the new situation.

   - You are not particularly happy about the new challenge but you realize you have to make some adjustments. You might not make a dramatic change, but you do enough to get by.

   - The new position requires you to develop some new techniques to be successful. You may not like the adjustment but you realize it is necessary in order to stay with a job you otherwise like.

4. **Change** and **adapt** your old skills so that they better fit the new demands.

   - You take the challenge head on. You may stumble a couple of times, but you make the needed changes in your skills to serve you better.

   - You want to thrive in the company and move up the promotion ladder. You search for ways to learn and grow each day.

It is possible for a student (or a worker) to go through all of these choices within a given situation. It can begin with the fear of a particularly challenging teacher at the beginning of the year—bringing on the desire to quit. You are not allowed to quit (by school administration, your parents, your financial aid requirements), so you stay in the class, dreading each day. Along the way, the teacher catches your attention, or another student helps you, or you have some inner change and you realize some adjustment must be made. Finally, you know you must completely modify your old skill so it works well with the new situation. (Strategies in these modules can help with this transformation.)

On the other hand, it may be a difficult supervisor. Do you quit the job, seek a transfer, or ignore the problem? The same skills apply.

You need to consciously identify and review at which level you are standing. First ask yourself, "Why?" Then ask yourself, "What can I do?" Sometimes, the first option—quit—is the best. You may be "overplaced" in a class (for example, you did not take a prerequisite course that taught the skills needed). Or the job is just not matched to your skills. But don't jump to this choice because it seems like the easy way out. Many times, quitting only postpones the inevitable; you will eventually need the skill in question. Let's examine Activity 1.3 to assess how you adapt old skills to new situations.

ACTIVITY 1.3 ASSESSMENT OF BROAD CHOICES

To reflect on the Success Strategy you read on page 10, complete the items below. Use the questions as guides. You do not need to answer each question.

1. When was the last time you either quit a situation (class or job, for instance) or seriously considered quitting a situation? What were the circumstances? Were there alternatives, such as seeking assistance or asking for clarification?

_____

_____

_____

_____

2. When was the last time you stayed in a miserable situation? What were the circumstances? Were there other alternatives? How did you feel?

_____

_____

_____

_____

3. When was the last time you made some minor adjustments to old skills in order to adjust to a new situation? What were the circumstances? Would you do it differently now?

_____

_____

_____

_____

4. When was the last time you made a major change to an old skill in order to be successful in a new situation? Would you be able to apply this change process to another situation in the future?

_____

_____

_____

_____

To help you reach an appropriate solution, here is a more specific six-point model to solve your problem.

Specific choices: The SAC-SIP problem-solving model

SUCCESS STRATEGY

(S) Stop. This is the easiest but most often overlooked step in problem solving. When confronted with a problem, stop and take a breath. This simple step allows your body to slow down and ready itself for a more considered opinion. Now you are ready to identify the problem. Before a problem can be solved, it has to be identified. Sounds obvious, doesn't it? Nevertheless, it is an often overlooked—and crucial—step. What exactly is the nature of the difficulty? Poor grades? Ineffective studying? A miserable supervisor? Or poor work habits?

(A) Alternatives. Once you have slowed down and identified the nature of the problem in front of you, then—and only then—can you start generating some ideas to address the challenge. Brainstorm potential avenues on which you can travel to the needed solution. Don't judge; just list possible alternatives.

(C) Consequences. Now that you have generated your potential solutions, take a moment and review what the consequences will be for each action. For instance, which of the solutions has the best result? Worst result? Is one riskier than another? Does each alternative address the problem you identified? Which ones can you tackle right now? Which ones ignore the problem?

(S) Select. Once you have critically evaluated the merits of each alternative, it is time to make a choice. Pick the best one and then make a plan to put it into action.

(I) Implement. Make a plan for how you will carry out the proposed solution. What is your first step? Second step? Last step?

(P) Pause. Take time to evaluate what you are doing. Is the plan working? Do you need to make adjustments?

Now let's take a look at Activity 1.4.

To reflect on the SAC-SIP problem-solving model, complete the items below. Work with a classmate and develop a creative plan.

(S) STOP. Think of a problem or a challenge you are having right now. Take a deep breath. Try to be as unemotional as you can about the issue. Close your eyes if you must; do whatever it takes to be able to focus analytically on the issue. What is the problem? Be careful to identify the problem, not the feeling associated with the problem. For instance, you might be failing a math course, and you don't like the instructor because you feel she is inattentive to your needs. Separate the two issues. It might be that you are failing because you are not prepared for the course. Or you might not like the teacher because you are failing the course. Or you are failing because the teacher has not been available to explain important concepts. Make a careful assessment and *determine what problem* you need to solve at this time.

_____

_____

_____

_____

(A) ALTERNATIVES. Now that you have identified what needs to be solved, brainstorm some ideas. Be creative at this step. You will make an objective and reasoned decision in the next step. Right now, you want to get possibilities on paper. If you censor yourself at this point, you may end up missing a quality solution.

1. _____

_____

2. _____

_____

3. _____

_____

(C) CONSEQUENCES. Take a moment and review what the consequences will be of each action. Which of the solutions has the best result? Worst result? Does each alternative address the problem you identified? Are the solutions strong? Which ones can you tackle right now? Which ones simply ignore the problem?

_____

_____

_____

_____

PUTTING THE SAC-SIP MODEL INTO ACTION, continued ACTIVITY **1.4**

(S) SELECTION. Now that you have your possible roads to the solution, objectively weigh the merits of each. Can any be eliminated because they are beyond your abilities? Do you have the resources (time, money, knowledge) to carry out the solutions? Which ones appeal to you? Which ones do not?

_____

_____

_____

_____

_____

(I) IMPLEMENT. Which option did you settle on? Why? How do you plan on carrying this out? What is your first step? Second step? Final step?

_____

_____

_____

_____

(P) PAUSE. When will you stop to evaluate your plan? How will you know if the plan is working or if it needs adjustment?

_____

_____

_____

_____

Case Study 1

Problem Solving

APPLYING YOUR NEW SKILLS TO THE WORKPLACE

SITUATION. Larry is a 26-year-old recent graduate of a small community college. While attending college, he maintained a 3.5 GPA, served on the student government as an officer, and held down a job in the campus mailroom. Staff and students liked him. He was always met with, "Hi, Larry! How are you doing?" Students came to him for advice, staff sought his input on issues, and the faculty held him up as a model student with award after award. Larry had a memorable college experience.

Larry greeted graduation day with a certain excitement. He had achieved his goals in college and now stood ready to tackle the world of work. He graduated on a Saturday and had a job waiting for him the following Monday. Life was good!

One week after graduation, Larry returns to campus to visit his former mailroom supervisor, Mrs. Carpenter. She is one of his most trusted mentors.

"Larry," exclaims Mrs. Carpenter, as he walks through the mailroom door. "What a pleasure to see you! Are you the president of the company yet?" She reaches out and gives him a heartfelt hug.

"Not only am I not the president, but I think I made a terrible mistake taking this job," says a dejected-looking Larry.

"Mistake? I don't understand." Mrs. Carpenter stands back and looks at Larry. "Come on, tell me. What's going on?"

"Well it's simply that I can't do the job," Larry explains. "I'm in an office with 30 other people. They've all been with the company for at least five years. I don't know which end is up! I'm lost. And nobody knows my name. I mean, they are nice and everything, but I get all of the boring stuff to do. I'm pretty much on my own." Larry plops down in a chair by her desk. "I'm going to quit on Monday."

Mrs. Carpenter doesn't say anything as she looks at Larry. He is so dejected it breaks her heart.

YOUR PROPOSED SOLUTION. How would you handle this? Why do you think Larry feels this way? Should he quit? How would you apply the *SAC-SIP* model here? What advice should Mrs. Carpenter give to Larry?

PROPOSED SOLUTION. Here is how Mrs. Carpenter utilizes the *SAC-SIP* method of problem solving.

Stop. Mrs. Carpenter takes Larry to the cafeteria for a cup of coffee. For a few moments, she reminisces about his accomplishments at the campus, which seems to calm him down. He trusts her. She finally gets him to identify the problem: *He is a rookie on the job. Few people know him. At college, he was a big fish in a small pond. Now, he is a faceless name in a big company. He has to prove himself all over again.*

Alternatives. Mrs. Carpenter gets Larry to see that quitting, although a quick remedy, is not the real solution. He is experiencing a typical reaction that many graduates feel as they move into a new situation. Over another cup of coffee, they brainstorm some alternatives.

Consequences. For each possible solution, they then discuss the possible results. Mrs. Carpenter gently leads Larry but she makes sure that he reaches the conclusions on his own.

Selection. Larry finally decides that quitting would not solve anything. After all, unless he wants to spend his whole life in the college mailroom, he will have to go through some kind of orientation period as a "rookie" in any job he chooses. He decides that he will seek out his current work supervisor, a kindly older man named Mr. Hopper, and see if he can establish a mentor relationship similar to what he has with Mrs. Carpenter.

Implementation. Larry decides he will meet with Mr. Hopper in the morning.

Pause. Mrs. Carpenter asks Larry to promise that he will come back to visit her in two weeks and report on his progress. Larry agrees.

YOUR REACTION TO THE PROPOSED SOLUTION. Will a mentor really make the difference? Is Larry just being a "baby" because he used to be such a big shot on campus? What other alternatives might you have suggested to Larry?

WHAT ARE STUDY SKILLS, AND WHY DO I NEED THEM?

Let's face it—given a choice of activities, reading a study skills book would probably not be a favorite for most people. But you have chosen to read this one, and that gives you a tremendous head start over someone with less motivation. You are about to embark on a journey—a journey that, frankly, is not for everyone. The modules in this book are for individuals interested in becoming successful students.

If you diligently review and practice the study skill strategies found in these modules, you will find that each step along the way prepares for exams. There is a continuous and flowing nature to these strategies. Once you understand and accept this fact, you will be well on your way to becoming the successful student you have always wanted to be. No more cramming.

Say good-bye to test anxiety. Welcome competence, confidence, and improved self-esteem.

What does a successful student look like?

Read and complete Activity 1.5.

ACTIVITY 1.5   EVALUATING THE CHARACTERISTICS OF A GOOD STUDENT

Read each of the following scenarios. After each description do the following: (1) Write whether or not you think the student is using effective study strategies, and (2) identify what is "good" and what the student could do better. After you have evaluated each description, share your thoughts with a classmate.

EXAMPLE 1: MIKE. Mike has a lot of homework to do for the evening. "I hate this stuff," he thinks. "It's so boring, boring, boring!" After 10 minutes of griping to himself, he sits on his bed, looks at the stack of books in front of him, and pulls out the closest one. It happens to be his history book. "Yuck! Who cares about what happened 300 years ago?" He opens the book to Chapter 14 and immediately starts reading. A few minutes later, he decides to flip on the radio for some background noise. As he returns to his book the phone rings. "Anything's better than this stuff," he groans, as he jumps up to answer the phone. Twenty-five minutes later, he finally finishes talking. He flips through the rest of the history book, looks at some of the pictures, and says to himself, "Professor Jones will never ask me a question anyway." He then moves on to his math homework. This course is giving him the most problems this year. "I need to be comfortable for this." He grabs his pillow, lies on his stomach, and starts flipping through the problems. He can't remember how the teacher did the problems today. He had copied similar problems from the board in class, but those are back at school in his notebook—which he left in the classroom. "Oh, well. I'll get the answers tomorrow from Tony." It is now about 15 minutes before Monday Night Football on TV. He looks at the science book. "Good," he thinks, "only five pages to read." With one eye on the clock and one eye on the book, he quickly scans the reading. "No problem. The test isn't until next week." At 9:00 P.M., he slams the book closed. "I've been studying for three hours. What else can they expect from me?" Time for a break.

Write your evaluation of Mike's study skills:

_____

_____

_____

_____

_____

_____

_____

EXAMPLE 2: BUBBA. Bubba has about two hours of homework ahead of him tonight. He sits at the kitchen table, takes out his assignment pad, and reviews his assignments. "It looks like math will take me about 45 minutes, the history reading about 30 minutes, the English grammar exercise only about 15 minutes, and the Spanish vocabulary—well, that's my toughest and it'll take a good 30 minutes to review," he says to himself. A bit reluctantly, he pulls out his Spanish flash cards and begins reviewing. "Might as well get this out of the way first," he thinks. Thirty minutes later, he takes a short break (5 minutes to get a glass of water and to stretch). He continues to work through his list, taking breaks every 25 or 30 minutes. He finishes his homework in time to play a computer game before going to bed.

Write your evaluation of Bubba's study skills:

_____

_____

_____

_____

_____

_____

_____

_____

EXAMPLE 3: LUCY. Lucy is having a tough year in school. It seems she is always behind. And each course is a struggle. "I'm doing a total of one hour of homework every night, but my grades sure don't reflect it! And those instructors do nothing but assign one project after another. My science research experiment is just around the corner. Thank goodness my outline is not due for another month," she says to herself. Tonight is one of those rare nights—no assigned homework. "I'm going to rest. I deserve it," she decides. With that, she turns on the TV and calls a friend.

Write your evaluation of Lucy's study skills:

_____

_____

_____

_____

_____

_____

_____

_____

Which student possesses the characteristics of a "successful student" or, in other words, a winning attitude? You may have identified some of the following study skills (or lack thereof):

MIKE

- *Poor attitude.* "I hate this stuff. . . . Yuck! . . . What else can they expect from me?"
- *Study space.* Given the little we know of Mike, it is questionable whether his bed is the best location to study. It just may be too comfortable.
- *Purpose in reading.* He immediately started reading his assignment. No warm-up, no skimming, no orientation as to what was important.
- *Distractions.* The radio and the phone don't seem to be ingredients of an effective study equation for Mike.
- *Lack of focus.* He "flipped through" his pages and quickly scanned "with one eye on the clock." Mike is not giving full attention to his work.
- *Timing.* Math is his most difficult course, yet he does not tackle it first when his energy level is (or should be) at its highest.
- *Academic tools.* Why is his math notebook not at home with him?
- *Realistic assessment.* Mike might have opened his books three hours before, but he certainly did not study for three hours. He is deluding himself.

BUBBA

- *Assignment pad.* Bubba has a written log of his homework. He can work from this to organize his studies for the evening.
- *Organized.* He takes a moment to map out the study schedule for the evening.
- *Priorities.* Bubba knows what subject causes him the most difficulties. He is going to focus his energies on this while he is the freshest.
- *Flash cards.* He has found a technique that helps him effectively store information.
- *Breaks.* He knows the power of taking a short time-out to "recharge his batteries."
- *Reward.* When Bubba completes his work, he takes time for himself to do something totally unrelated to academics. Not only is he signaling an end to the day's studies, but he is also providing balance for his life.

LUCY

- *Always behind.* The question has to be, *Why* is Lucy always behind? Is she giving enough effort? Does she stay current with reading and class work? Is she overplaced; that is, is she in the right class?
- *One hour of homework.* By the time one gets to college, one hour of homework is definitely not a burden. In fact, middle school students have that much, if not more. While the "formula" might be old, it is still appropriate to plan on two to three hours of out-of-class preparation for each hour in class.

- *Attitude.* Stop blaming the instructors. Accept responsibility.

- *No assigned homework.* Really? Has she reviewed her notes from the day (does she have any notes from the day)? What about future projects? Any steps to be taken now? And if she is always behind, might this not be a great night to try to catch up?

- *Procrastination.* The science project is due in a month. Why not accomplish a small step toward its completion.

- *Attitude, again.* "I'm going to rest. I deserve it." Sounds like she has been doing quite a bit of resting!

What you need to do to be a successful student

SUCCESS STRATEGY

Successful students are not necessarily the students who study the most or who have the highest IQs. The so-called smart students are successful students who have mastered the art of *focusing*. These students have learned how to accomplish quality schoolwork in shorter periods—leaving time for personal, nonacademic goals. More specifically, successful students are those students who

- focus on the *connection* between strengths and challenges. Too many times, students only look at their weaknesses. Be sure to look at your strengths as well.

- focus on *desire.* You are the one responsible for good grades. Yes, you have teachers, but you have to have the will to be successful. Without this drive and motivation, you might as well put this book down now and turn on the television. As the army motto goes, "Be all you can be!"

- focus on *responsibility.* You are responsible for yourself. Successful students know they need *to act on their environment,* rather than constantly reacting *to what happens to them.* You might not be able to control everything that comes your way, but with a little work, you will be able to minimize the times you cry out, "Why is this happening to me?"

- focus on *attitude.* Successful students *want* to be successful students. Change the way you look at yourself. Get rid of negative thoughts about yourself. This is a major premise of this book.

- focus on being an *active learner.* Use as much of your brain as possible. One study skills teacher[2] maintains that we only use 3 percent of our brain. Think about that. It has also been said that the brain is capable of handling about 600 words per minute; most people speak at about 125 words per minute.[3] What does that mean for the student in the classroom? Drifting attention may very well indicate that you have a normally active brain, but remember our major purpose—you want to be successful, so you need to channel that activity in a positive manner.

- focus on *achievement*—the added edge needed for academic excellence. There is competition in school. It is in the classroom, in the ability to

---

[2]Claude W. Olney, *Where There's a Will There's an "A"* (Paoli, PA: Chesterbrook Educational Publishers, 1990), videocassette.

[3]Henry E. Florey, Jr. *Study Orientation Skills: Participant Manual* (Tuscaloosa, AL: Author, 1987), 21.

achieve a spot on the drama squad or the athletic team, or admission to the school of your choice.

- focus on *mastery*. One of the best ways to achieve confidence in your abilities is to master the tasks before you. That takes all of the above: connection, desire, responsibility, attitude, active learning, and achievement. Mastery leads to confidence, which will build self-esteem.

A word about self-esteem

What helps build positive self-esteem? Warm strokes are nice, but they can end up being empty. For example, if you turn in a poorly written essay and the teacher wants to "spare your feelings," he can write all sorts of nice comments on your paper (such as "I like your penmanship"). However, this type of compliment is useless for success, because it has nothing to do with the task; the skill has not been mastered.

One more thing about self-esteem: Handling criticism

Criticism is part of education. Whether you want to call it evaluation, or judgment, or grading, or feedback, it is all criticism of your work in one form or another. "Okay, but what does this have to do with study skills?" you might ask. Whether fair or not, there is nothing like someone's critical comments to bring us to a sobering reality about our abilities. How you handle the criticism can have an impact on your attitude and view of your classroom potential.

SUCCESS STRATEGY

When evaluating and responding to criticism you should consider two factors: the *motivation* of the person criticizing and the *soundness* of the criticism.

Motivation. Your teachers will be giving you *constructive criticism*. This can still sting but the intent is clearly to help you improve. Even if the criticism is inaccurate, the critic is well meaning. The kind of criticism you want to be aware of is *manipulative criticism*. In this case, the criticizer has some (conscious or unconscious) other desire (such as to get you to do something for him or her).

Soundness. Before you blow up in the professor's face, you may wish to evaluate the criticism. Is it accurate? You may not *like* it but that does not mean the evaluation of your latest essay is not accurate. Even if you come to the reasoned conclusion that the criticism is unfounded, make a measured response. If you are too upset to respond at that time, politely ask if you may have time to review the comments on your paper and come back later to discuss the issue. Time has a way of providing objectivity that the emotions of the moment might cloud.

Well-motivated and accurate criticism provides an essential step as you learn from mistakes. It is part of the learning process.

Practicing a skill will develop a certain level of competence. Competence leads to confidence—and it is difficult for a confident individual to have poor self-esteem.

SUCCESS STRATEGY

Case Study 2

Handling Criticism

SITUATION. "Whew! Will I ever be glad when this project is completed," Laurie sighs to herself as she turns off her computer for the day.

For the better part of the last two days, she has been putting together the agenda for tomorrow's meeting with the board of directors. This is the first time Laurie is in charge of all the details of the meeting. She has observed a couple of these gatherings in the past, but she quickly finds out that *observing* and *organizing* are two different things.

Laurie's boss, Debra, gave Laurie the assignment at the last minute due to staffing problems in the office. On her way out of the office this particular evening, Laurie pokes her head in Debra's office.

"Well, everything is set for the big meeting tomorrow, boss," Laurie says with a smile.

Debra looks up from a pile of papers she is reading and says, "Good. This is an important meeting. We will be looking at the budget figures for next year. You did bind the information in three-ring binders for all of the directors, didn't you?"

Laurie's face flushes and she stammers, "N-n-no. I thought that was taken care of. I thought I was just to get the agenda printed, contact the directors and remind them of the meeting, and . . ."

"Laurie, the purpose of the budget meeting is to discuss the budget. I will lead the discussion. In fact, I will handle most of the meeting. But you know I don't have time to get the handouts ready for everyone. Also, you did order the food, didn't you?" Debra looks at Laurie expectantly.

On the inside Laurie is screaming, "Food! What, am I a waitress?" But on the outside she says, "No, I didn't know that was my job either." She tries to remain calm, but it's not easy.

Debra slides back in her chair. "Look, I know you've been getting all of the little details together. They are important, but this isn't a sorority social that we are putting on. Anytime there is a board of directors meeting, everything has to be planned to the last detail. There can be no room for error. These are important people with tight schedules and lots of influence in the community. We don't want to look like amateurs." Debra doesn't yell. In fact, she speaks in a calm, measured tone, but her displeasure is evident. "The meeting is at 9:00 A.M. You will need to have the budget notebooks in place by then. If you call Tony's Café now, they will be able to get biscuits, rolls, and coffee here by 8:30. Here's the phone number."

Laurie takes the business card from Debra and looks at it. Debra goes back to reading her papers. Laurie turns and leaves, her mind spinning with all sorts of thoughts. Most of all she is angry that she has been chastised. She believes she did everything asked of her. Yes, she had been to other meetings, but doesn't Debra realize this is her first time organizing it?

"This is the thanks I get! No appreciation. Just criticism! Why doesn't she just do it herself if I'm so bad?" Laurie says to herself as she heads back to her office.

YOUR PROPOSED SOLUTION. Why do you think Laurie reacted as she did? Is she justified? Should she have said anything to the boss about all of the work she had done? Should she have protested? Should she have been more forceful and

revealed her feelings rather than holding them inside? What about her assessment that she is "bad"? How should she proceed from this point?

PROPOSED SOLUTION. Laurie's reaction is understandable. After all, she had worked on the project, done what she thought was appropriate, only to be told she had missed some major points. But she should step back for a moment and review the criticism that Debra directed her way.

Stop.   When she gets to her office, Laurie paces back and forth for a few moments. She is still upset. She takes a deep breath and decides to sit down and survey the situation.

Laurie reviews in her mind what Debra said about her deficiencies in planning the board meeting. She has to admit, Debra is correct. There are some glaring omissions. Laurie realizes that she needs to address these deficiencies immediately, so she works an hour and a half extra in order to be prepared for the meeting first thing in the morning. During this time, her coworker, Nick, stops in to say good night. Laurie tells him what happened.

"I understand why she said what she said," explains Laurie, "but I'm still upset by the criticism."

Alternatives.   "I understand," Nick says with a nod. "The same kind of thing has happened to me before. I worked my tail off and then caught criticism. Darn frustrating! But you need to figure out how to deal with it."

"I know, but how?" asks Laurie.

"The way I see it, you have three options," Nick says. "One, you can ignore it, go about your business, and make believe the criticism never happened. Two, you can march right down to Debra's office and assertively tell her you disagree with the criticism. Or three, you can try to figure out what motivated the criticism and determine if it was accurate or not."

Consequences.   "I don't particularly like either option one or two," responds Laurie. "In the first case, ignoring it will not help me deal with the problem. It will probably just continue to bother me. The second option doesn't seem to be the politically correct thing to do. And she did have a point."

Selection.   "Your third choice is the one I need to embrace if I want a future with this company," continues Laurie. "Can you help me analyze this, Nick?"

Implementation.   With Nick's guidance, Laurie tries to look objectively at the motivation and accuracy of the criticism. Here is what she determines.

Motivation.   Debra did not criticize Laurie. She criticized the incomplete job. Yes, maybe Debra should have been more specific in her details, but Debra is the boss putting together the major presentation for the meeting. Laurie, as her assistant, needs to be as thorough as possible. Debra did not deliver a mean-spirited attack. There was no manipulation; it was a direct evaluation of a job that was incomplete.

Soundness.   Laurie felt slighted. It's true that the job was incomplete. But it's also true that she did not get much direction due to the staffing problems in the office.

Pause.   Laurie decides that the next morning, after the board meeting, she will set up a meeting with Debra to discuss how she feels about the criticism and why she had gone about the planning the way she had.

YOUR REACTION TO THE PROPOSED SOLUTION. What do you think of Laurie's solution? Is it important for her to tell her boss how she feels? Or would it be more appropriate just to get the assistance she needs for future meetings? Should she even meet with her boss about the issue? Will Laurie look weak or complaining?

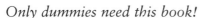

What do you think of when you hear the term *study skills?*

Most students approach a study skills course (or book) with little or no enthusiasm. It's not one of the most popular topics in the course catalog. Typical responses include

> *Only dummies need this book!*
>
> *Why do I need this course? I do my homework every night. Isn't that studying?*
>
> *What makes smart students smart? How do they do it? They must do nothing but homework—bunch of nerds!*
>
> *My adviser made me take this course.*
>
> *My mother made me take this course.*

Interestingly enough, good grades do *not* have to be accompanied by long hours of work. I have seen very capable students "overdo it" on homework. It is possible to overstudy, become stressed, and waste your energies. I'm not advocating that you stop working, just that you work more effectively. Here's an example.

Have you ever studied for a long time only to be baffled by a large red *F* on an exam? How frustrating. Many students complain, "I sat at that desk for hours last night—and I still bombed!"

Given a list of tasks to remember, people will tend to remember best the first thing/group and the last thing/group of that list.[4] The student who decides to study three hours, without a break, for an exam will more than likely remember what he or she studied at the very beginning of the study time and at the very end. Retention of the material in the middle is more questionable.

Try, as Dr. Olney suggests, breaking up your study period into, say, three one-hour blocks of time. Now, instead of just one start and one end there are three starts and three ends. If his original premise is correct, you are more likely to remember six groups of items rather than just two.

So, an important strategy is to give yourself a break when studying. Be reasonable and moderate in your approach. A related strategy is to give yourself an *appropriate* reward at each brief break. For instance, after one hour of reviewing your reading assignment, you can get a snack, or listen to five minutes of music, or just walk outside and play with the dog for a couple of

---

[4]See Olney. Also, see Roger G. Swartz, *Accelerated Learning: How You Learn Determines What You Learn* (Durant, OK: EMIS, 1991), 61. Swartz states, "A decline in recall occurs, especially for material studied during the mid-point of the process, if study periods are too lengthy."

minutes. The point is to stay fresh and alert. *More* is not necessarily *better*. Examine the following two options.

Option 1.   You start studying at 7:00 P.M. and stop at 10:00 P.M. During this time you take no breaks, so you wind up studying for three straight hours. Therefore, there is one start point and one stop point. That means there are *two groups of information* that will more likely be remembered.

OR

Option 2.   You start studying at 7:00 P.M. and stop at 10:00 P.M. This time you study for one hour at a time followed by a five-minute break. Thus, there are three starts and three stops during this study period. That means there are *six groups of remembered information.*

Which method do you think is more effective?

If you allow breaks in your schedule, homework will be less tedious. You also will have much more time left for studying.

"Wait a minute," I can hear you say. "I thought I *was* just studying for three hours!" Well, maybe you were and maybe you weren't. Students who excel know that doing nightly homework is not necessarily studying. Doing math problems, reading a history assignment, or completing a grammar exercise is not studying.

If completing an assignment is not studying, what is?

The first time you are introduced to material, you are simply becoming familiar with the concepts. When you start reviewing and relating this material *then* you are studying. You will learn more about this in later modules. For the moment, understand that those successful students sitting next to you in class know *how* to study. It's not magic—you can do it too.

SUCCESS STRATEGY

Smart students know their challenges. I have worked with high-IQ students who were *not* very smart. *Smart* means to be *shrewd*, which means to have *keen insight*. The point here is to know your strengths and weaknesses. Challenges may vary, but all of us must face them.

Remember the major premise of this book: how to be a successful student. Now, what can *you* do about these challenges?

The skills and strategies to overcome your challenges go beyond the classroom. Think of something you want in your personal life (make a sports team, meet a new friend, go to a particular concert). How would you go about accomplishing the task?

One last thing: A covenant with myself

Since this journey is all about you—your desire, your needs, your success—take a moment and complete the covenant in Exhibit 1.1. Let me point out two things about this document:

- This is a *covenant* as opposed to a *contract*. The term *contract* too often has connotations of distrust: "I'm not sure you will do what you say; therefore, I want you to sign this contract." I would like to use a much

An example of a covenant. *exhibit 1.1*

COVENANT WITH MYSELF

I, _____, pledge myself to try my best as I work through these modules. I will complete all activities honestly and thoughtfully. I will have an open mind and I will follow through on all activities as instructed. I will actively participate in class discussions and group activities. I will seek assistance as needed, and I will be ready to lend a hand to fellow students who may have difficulties with the activities and strategies. (After all, teaching is sometimes the best way to learn a new skill.) I will apply these strategies, as appropriate, in my other classes, as well as in my life beyond the campus. In short, I pledge to focus my energies as best I can.

Date: _____   Signature: _____

more positive approach. A *covenant* implies respect and trust. It is a public proclamation of that respect.

- This covenant is strictly personal. It is a compact you will make with yourself. If you don't follow through, you don't follow through with yourself. Your signature indicates your desire to improve, your respect for yourself, and the trust you place in your abilities to do the best you can.

A QUICK REVIEW

Whether you are tackling a reading assignment, doing a research paper, or completing an exam, it is critical to have an overview of material before you. Exhibit 1.2 is a graphic representation of the material in these modules. Notice how each skill topic is connected to another.

Complete the following exercises.

1. List five of the top 10 challenges all students must face:
   A. _____
   B. _____
   C. _____
   D. _____
   E. _____

exhibit 1.2   A graphic representation of the topics in this book.

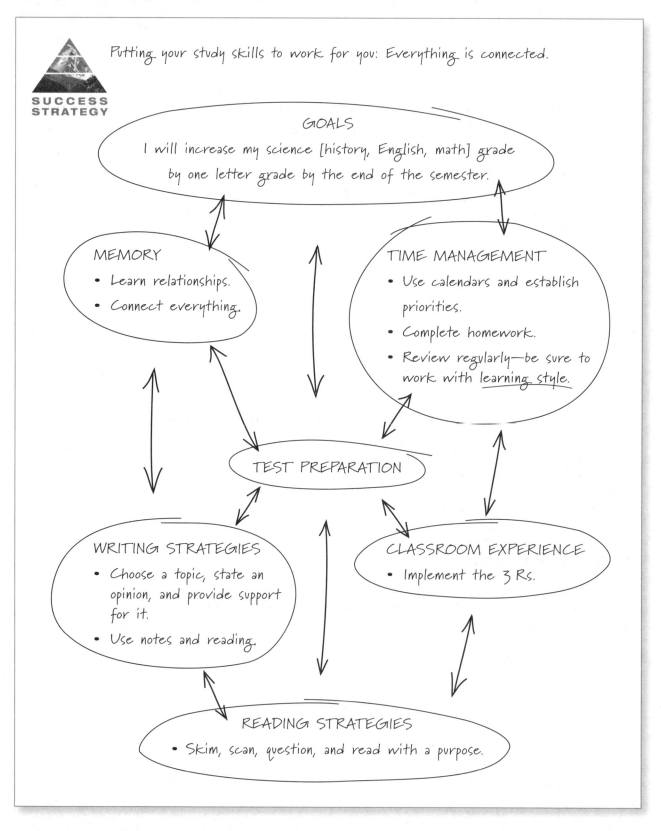

SUCCESS STRATEGY

Putting your study skills to work for you: Everything is connected.

GOALS
I will increase my science [history, English, math] grade by one letter grade by the end of the semester.

MEMORY
- Learn relationships.
- Connect everything.

TIME MANAGEMENT
- Use calendars and establish priorities.
- Complete homework.
- Review regularly—be sure to work with learning style.

TEST PREPARATION

WRITING STRATEGIES
- Choose a topic, state an opinion, and provide support for it.
- Use notes and reading.

CLASSROOM EXPERIENCE
- Implement the 3 Rs.

READING STRATEGIES
- Skim, scan, question, and read with a purpose.

2. What are the four broad choices you have when trying to match old skills to new situations?

_____

_____

_____

_____

3. List and briefly explain each of the steps of the SAC-SIP problem-solving model.

_____

_____

_____

_____

4. When evaluating someone's criticism of your actions, what are the two things you should take into consideration?

_____

_____

_____

_____

5. What will you do to make sure you keep the "Covenant with myself"?

_____

_____

_____

_____

Now, it's time to dig in and make that commitment to academic success. Pick the module or modules that will best suit your purposes and then start the transformation process. Best wishes.

LEARNING STYLES AND MULTIPLE INTELLIGENCES

*I don't learn like you,
you don't learn like me.*

"Far better it is
to dare mighty things,
to win glorious triumphs,
even though checkered
with failure, than
to take rank with
those poor spirits
who neither
enjoy much nor
suffer much,

because they live in
the gray twilight that
knows not victory
nor defeat."

—THEODORE ROOSEVELT,
TWENTY-SIXTH PRESIDENT
OF THE UNITED STATES

MODULE 2

Overview of This Module

LEARNING STYLES

One size does not fit all

Imagine this. You walk into a doctor's office and announce, "Doc, I don't feel well. Fix me." Any reasonable doctor would first need to know some specifics: What are your symptoms? What medications are you currently taking? To what drugs are you allergic?

In other words, the doctor has to recognize you as an individual patient with distinct and separate characteristics from other patients in the waiting room. The same goes for study skills. You are a unique student. A prescribed study skill for a classmate might not be appropriate for you.

These modules provide many suggestions. You need to *concentrate on those that fit your learning style best.* (This isn't permission to reject those strategies that seem to be too much work. Many will require some additional effort at first.) Be mindful of how you learn. You should be aware of the conditions that work best for you: absolute quiet or quiet background noise, structure or flexibility, solitude or group interaction.

A word of warning. Just because you *do* something now when you study, does *not* mean it is your learning style. It might be your *preference*—what you like—but that does not mean it is how you *learn.* If we are honest with ourselves, we will probably find that many habits are not very productive to task accomplishment. I have heard students proudly state, "I can study while watching the football game." In reality, they are going through the motions of studying. The quality of learning taking place under these conditions is questionable at best.

How do *you* learn?

Very simply, "learning style" refers to the manner in which individuals process information.[1] This module is not, nor does it attempt to be, the definitive source on learning styles. My purpose is to raise your level of awareness about *your* style. I want you to become more in tune with the best way you learn. The material in this section just scratches the surface of a large body of research.

Take a moment and complete the inventory in Activity 2.1. Keep in mind that this is not a scientific instrument; it is simply a reflective method for you to become more sensitive to what does and does not work for you.

Various factors, from the environment to the manner of presentation by the teacher, affect us differently. Some of the environmental factors that affect learning include

- food and drink.
- light.
- sound.
- temperature.
- comfort of furniture.
- structure of time and/or task.
- ability to move about.
- peer interaction.

When it comes to teacher presentation, we all have a particular style that helps us best understand and process the material being presented. For instance, some of us can listen to a *verbal* explanation of a task and then carry out the assignment successfully. In this case, we receive *auditory* directions and translate them into a product.

Others (myself included) must *see* something before we can process it. For example, if I have to install a computer program, it is very helpful for me to see diagrammed instructions. Simple word directions would be more difficult for me to process. *Visual* aids greatly enhance my ability to learn.

Still others work best by *physically manipulating* objects. A student who is better able to understand a biological principle after a laboratory experiment learns processing in a *kinesthetic* (or body movement) manner.

Now turn to Activity 2.2 to evaluate your particular learning style.

---

[1] A great deal has been written about learning styles. My intent here is to provide a brief overview. For more information see Nancy Lightfoot Matte and Susan Hillary Henderson, *Success Your Style: Right- and Left-Brain Techniques for Learning* (Belmont, CA: Wadsworth, 1995); Rita Dunn and Kenneth Dunn, *Teaching Students Through Their Individual Learning Styles: A Practical Approach* (Reston, VA: Reston Publishing, 1978); Roger G. Swartz, *Accelerated Learning: How You Learn Determines What You Learn* (Durant, OK: EMIS, 1991); James Keefe, *Learning Style Handbook: II. Accommodating Perceptual, Study and Instructional Preferences* (Reston, VA: National Association of Secondary School Principals, 1989); and David Lazear, *Seven Ways of Knowing: Teaching for Multiple Intelligences* (Palatine, IL: Skylight, 1991).

ACTIVITY 2.1   HOW DO I LEARN BEST?

Check the items that apply to you. When choosing, remember to ask yourself, "Is this what produces the best results for me?"

When studying, I *most often do best* when . . .

- ○ 1. The room is brightly lit.
- ○ 2. The room is lit by one light at my study area.
- ○ 3. The room is colder than it is warm.
- ○ 4. The room is warmer than it is cold.
- ○ 5. I sit in a hard, straight-backed chair at a desk.
- ○ 6. I sit in a comfortable chair at a desk.
- ○ 7. I recline on the floor.
- ○ 8. I schedule time for schoolwork.
- ○ 9. I hear things rather than read things.
- ○ 10. I see things rather than hear them.
- ○ 11. Someone explains a process to me.
- ○ 12. I can physically assemble something myself.
- ○ 13. I move around the room.
- ○ 14. I sit on the edge of my chair.
- ○ 15. I have just finished a meal.
- ○ 16. It is early in the day.
- ○ 17. It is late in the day.
- ○ 18. I work by myself.
- ○ 19. I work in groups.
- ○ 20. I take breaks.
- ○ 21. I sit for long periods, without a break, and completely finish a project.
- ○ 22. There are very few distractions.
- ○ 23. There is soft background noise.
- ○ 24. There is loud music.
- ○ 25. There is absolute quiet.
- ○ 26. I draw illustrations to accompany the material I am learning.
- ○ 27. I hold something (a rubber ball, a small beanbag) while studying.
- ○ 28. I do an experiment rather than write a paper.
- ○ 29. I explain new concepts to my friends.
- ○ 30. I quickly survey an assignment so that I can see what is coming.

○ 31. I am quizzed by a parent, friend, or roommate.

○ 32. I can watch a movie of a novel I have just read.

○ 33. There is an open window for fresh air.

○ 34. I have no set study time.

○ 35. I read aloud when completing a reading assignment.

○ 36. I associate a picture with the name of a personality or an event.

○ 37. Someone constantly reminds me of deadlines and structure.

○ 38. I am allowed to be curious and explore without rigid guidelines.

○ 39. I know exactly what is expected.

○ 40. I can take risks.

○ 41. Things are presented in an ordered or chronological fashion.

○ 42. List any other characteristics that apply to your learning style:

_____

_____

_____

_____

_____

_____

_____

ACTIVITY 2.2 WHAT IS MY LEARNING STYLE?

Next to each of the four categories below, write the numbers of the items you checked in Activity 2.1 that seem to correspond to that category. Do you find that one or more categories have the most numbers or are they "spread out" over several categories?

Auditory: learn best by hearing _____

Kinesthetic: learn best by doing, touching, and moving _____

Visual: learn best by seeing _____

Environmental: impact of the surroundings on your learning _____

What conclusions can you draw about your style? Write a brief description of the manner in which you learn. How do you know this is accurate? List as many specific examples from your academic experience that support your conclusion.

_____

_____

_____

_____

_____

_____

_____

_____

_____

_____

_____

_____

SUCCESS STRATEGY

How does this information help me?

If you have difficulties in the classroom, they may not be due to a lack of effort on your part. The problem might be related to how you are processing information. Using the four categories described in Activity 2.2, you can develop a better understanding of the style and setting in which you learn best. To reinforce this, Modules 3 through 9 end with suggested connections to learning styles. Feel free to add as benefits your style.

WHAT ARE MULTIPLE INTELLIGENCES?

Whereas *learning style* looks at *how* we learn, *intelligence* refers to our abilities to *solve* problems. Much work has been done recently in the area of multiple intelligences. This theory addresses "the broad range of abilities that humans possess by grouping their capabilities into [multiple] comprehensive categories of intelligence."[2] While nothing so profound is attempted here, I would like to give a brief overview of this concept.

Howard Gardner, a Harvard professor, did pioneering research in this area. He maintains that measuring intelligence (IQ) with one number is misleading. It leads us to believe that there is *one* intelligence. According to Dr. Gardner, there are actually eight intelligences.[3] That is, we have eight different abilities to pick from when solving problems. Unfortunately, many of us have been trained to use only two or three of these. Just think of what we can do once we tap into as many of the eight intelligences as possible!

The eight intelligences[4]

Although some of the eight intelligences are more advanced than the others, we have traces of each intelligence. Some may be highly developed and some a little less developed. Here is Gardner's list (with clarification in parentheses provided from the work of Thomas Armstrong[5]).

Linguistic intelligence (word smart). You are good with the written word. You can express yourself with language. Occupations include writer, speaker, lawyer, and teacher.

---

[2]Thomas Armstrong, *Multiple Intelligences in the Classroom* (Alexandria, VA: Association for Supervision and Curriculum Development, 1994), p. 2. Armstrong, in a very straightforward manner, describes and analyzes the first seven intelligences identified by Howard Gardner. The descriptions of the intelligences contained here come from an interview of Howard Gardner found in Kathy Checkley, "The First Seven . . . and the Eighth: A Conversation with Howard Gardner," *Educational Leadership* [online], Association for Curriculum and Development, 55, no. 1, September 1997; available from www.ascd.org/readingroom/edlead/9709/checkley.html). Accessed December 15, 2002.

[3]Gardner's groundbreaking book is entitled *Frames of Mind: The Theory of Multiple Intelligences* (1993).

[4]A ninth intelligence is being investigated—spiritual. This intelligence refers to the ability to connect with nonphysical or metaphysical stimuli. For our purposes we will look at the first eight.

[5]See Armstrong 1994 for more detailed information.

Logical-mathematical intelligence (number smart). You can think abstractly and solve problems. Logic and order are strengths for you. You understand cause and effect. Manipulation of numbers comes easily. Occupations include scientist and mathematician.

Spatial intelligence (art smart). You can re-create your world visually. A sound sense of direction is involved, too. Occupations include sculptor, painter, and anatomy teacher.

Bodily-kinesthetic intelligence (body smart). You have coordinated control of your own body. There is a strong sense of learning by movement or action. You can effectively use your hands, fingers, and arms to make something. Occupations include athlete, actor, and dancer.

Musical intelligence (music smart). You have the ability to use the major components of music (rhythm or pitch). You can recognize patterns and use them effectively. Occupations include musician and dancer.

Interpersonal intelligence (people smart). You have an understanding of the mood and motives of those with whom you associate. If you are to effectively deal with other people you must be skilled in this intelligence. Occupations include teacher, politician, and salesperson.

Intrapersonal intelligence (me smart). You understand yourself and can apply that knowledge in real-life situations to produce the best results. You understand what is good for you. You know who you are and what you can do. You know what to associate with and what to avoid. Occupations include independent contractor.

Naturalistic intelligence (nature smart). You can understand, explain, and relate to things in the natural world around you. You have a unique ability to classify and separate items based on characteristics. Occupations include botanist, zoologist, archaeologist, and environmentalist.

If you can understand what your dominant intelligences are, you will be better equipped to tackle challenges—and they may even give you a window into future life choices. The occupations listed with each type of intelligence are just a sampling of the many careers from which you will be able to choose.

Activity 2.3 will help you to prioritize *your* intelligences. Once you have finished Activity 2.3, have a friend complete Activity 2.4. Ask him or her to rate you on the same intelligences—but don't show what you have written.

PRIORITIZING YOUR INTELLIGENCES ACTIVITY 2.3

Review the list of multiple intelligences one more time. Now list the intelligences in order of strongest (the one intelligence that is most developed) to least (the one that is least developed) as they relate to you. Briefly describe why you believe this. Be specific (perhaps give an example that proves your ranking).

My most developed intelligence is _____.

My evidence is _____

_____

_____

_____

_____

My second most developed intelligence is _____.

My evidence is _____

_____

_____

_____

_____

My third most developed intelligence is _____.

My evidence is _____

_____

_____

_____

_____

My fourth most developed intelligence is _____.

My evidence is _____

_____

_____

_____

_____

(continued)

My fifth most developed intelligence is _____ .

My evidence is _____

_____

_____

_____

_____

My sixth most developed intelligence is _____ .

My evidence is _____

_____

_____

_____

_____

My seventh most developed intelligence is _____ .

My evidence is _____

_____

_____

_____

_____

My eighth most developed intelligence is _____ .

My evidence is _____

_____

_____

_____

_____

A FRIEND'S REVIEW OF YOUR INTELLIGENCES

Now that you have described yourself, use the following to ask a friend to do the same. Sometimes others see characteristics and strengths that we miss in ourselves. Compare the responses of your friend's review to what you wrote in your descriptions.

My friend's most developed intelligence is _____.

My evidence is _____

_____

_____

_____

_____

My friend's second most developed intelligence is _____.

My evidence is _____

_____

_____

_____

_____

My friend's third most developed intelligence is _____.

My evidence is _____

_____

_____

_____

_____

My friend's fourth most developed intelligence is _____.

My evidence is _____

_____

_____

_____

_____

(continued)

ACTIVITY 2.4   A FRIEND'S REVIEW OF YOUR INTELLIGENCES, continued

My friend's fifth most developed intelligence is _____ .

My evidence is _____

_____

_____

_____

_____

My friend's sixth most developed intelligence is _____ .

My evidence is _____

_____

_____

_____

_____

My friend's seventh most developed intelligence is _____ .

My evidence is _____

_____

_____

_____

_____

My friend's eighth most developed intelligence is _____ .

My evidence is _____

_____

_____

_____

_____

SUCCESS STRATEGY

Okay, what does all this mean to me?

The intent is not to give you a rigid label. There will be times when you learn very well by visual means, and times when auditory techniques are more productive. There will be times when your "word smart" stands out above all else, and at other times, you will exhibit great spatial capabilities. Individual work might be your normal routine, but a study group can be appropriate when trying to understand a troubling concept. The point is to understand what works best *most of the time*. Then use that knowledge for your benefit.

For instance, if you are "word smart," take advantage of that talent and use the note-taking strategy (TSD[6] method) introduced in Module 5, "The Classroom Experience." Reorganize your notes so they make sense to you.

As you proceed through these modules, keep your learning style(s) in mind. For example, a "visual" student might have more success with the "flow chart" format found in Module 5 than the traditional outline. Although this will be emphasized in each module, an ongoing assignment is to be vigilant as you read. What strategies fit your style of processing information? Knowing this will engage you as an active, rather than a passive, learner. More important, it will give *you* more control of *your* academic process and progress.

Understanding your learning styles is one more tool in your book bag to combat poor school performance. Use the knowledge productively. (Note, however, that in this book I do not address specific learning disabilities.)

Why don't you *become* the teacher?

Many books address the topic of multiple intelligences. Teachers have attended many workshops on how to use this teaching tool to help their students.

In Gardner's own words:

> What I argue against is the notion that there's only one way to learn and how to read, only one way to learn how to compute, only one way to learn about biology. . . . The point is to realize that any topic of importance, from any discipline, can be taught in more than one way.[7]

Nevertheless, you still may run into teachers who are not versed in this theory. Don't despair. Exhibit 2.1 helps you to become your own teacher.

---

[6]TSD stands for *title, summary, details* as they apply to class notes.

[7]See Checkley.

exhibit 2.1 How to complement selected intelligences.

WHEN GIVEN AN ASSIGNMENT OR TASK, IF YOU ARE STRONG IN . . .	THEN ASK YOURSELF . . .
Linguistic intelligence	"How can I use language (written or spoken) to help me with this task?"
Logical-mathematical intelligence	"How can I use numbers, logic, or manipulations to help me with this task?"
Spatial intelligence	"How can I use visualization, aids, color, or art to help me with this task?"
Bodily-kinesthetic intelligence	"How can I use body movement or manipulate the environment to help me with this task?"
Musical intelligence	"How can I use music or patterns to help me with this task?"
Interpersonal intelligence	"How can I use my knowledge of and skill in dealing with other people to help me with this task?"
Intrapersonal intelligence	"How can I use my self-knowledge to help me with this task?"
Naturalistic intelligence	"How can I use my ability to classify and categorize the environment to help me with this task?"

A QUICK REVIEW

The topic of study skills is more than spending hours and hours staring at a pile of books and homework assignments. It is about

- studying efficiently and effectively.
- combining practical skills with potential and desire.
- combining competence with responsibility.
- practicing new strategies.
- being organized.
- implementing strategies that fit your own learning style.
- being in control of your academic progress.

Complete the following exercises.

1. Which choice describes *learning style?*
   A. how teachers prefer their students to learn
   B. how individuals process information
   C. an individual's IQ
   D. a style that is similar for same-age students

2. What three environmental factors could affect your academic productivity?

   A. _____

   B. _____

   C. _____

3. What is the connection between the concepts of *learning styles* and *study skills?*

   _____

   _____

   _____

   _____

4. If you are good with the written word, you are exhibiting which of the multiple intelligences?

   A. spatial intelligence

   B. linguistic intelligence

   C. musical intelligence

   D. naturalistic intelligence

5. What is the difference between *learning styles* and *multiple intelligences?*

   _____

   _____

   _____

   _____

   _____

   _____

Checklist

Checklist of Selected Tips and Strategies

As a last review, collaborate with a classmate and write a brief description of how each of the following will help you become a more successful student.

LEARNING STYLES AND MULTIPLE INTELLIGENCES

1. Identifying learning styles

_____

_____

_____

2. Connecting between strengths and challenges

_____

_____

_____

3. Having competence and self-esteem

_____

_____

_____

4. Understanding each of the multiple intelligences

_____

_____

_____

5. Knowing how learning styles and multiple intelligences differ

_____

_____

_____

GOAL SETTING

Knowing where you are going and how best to get there

"Destiny is no matter of chance. It is a matter of choice. It is not a thing to be waited for. It is a thing to be achieved."

—WILLIAM JENNINGS BRYAN, POLITICIAN, LAWYER, AND PRESIDENTIAL CANDIDATE IN 1896

MODULE 3

Overview of This Module

MOTIVATIONAL GOAL SETTING

I don't have time for this stuff!

"Meaningful specific" or "wandering generality": Goals provide direction

What does a clearly stated goal look like?

W.I.N.: Do you know what's important now?

Evaluate your goals: "Wanting" to do something is not the same thing as "doing" something

A QUICK REVIEW

MOTIVATIONAL GOAL SETTING

If you wanted to become a member of an athletic team, earn first chair in the school band, or win the lead in this year's drama production, how would you go about it? That is, how would you achieve your desired end? If you want to be successful, you will have to establish your goal ("I want to win the lead part in the drama production") and then identify the steps you need to address in order to attain that goal ("I will attend auditions, project my voice, exude confidence, and rehearse the script").

When it comes to success in the classroom, the same process should be used. What, after all, is more motivating than establishing what you want to achieve and then pursuing that dream? You have to visualize your success. The first step is to establish a clearly stated plan of *what* you want, *when* you want it, and *how* you are going to get there. Goals need to be personal—not someone else's idea of what you should accomplish.

If you want someone else to run your life, skip this module and move on to the next one.

SUCCESS
STRATEGY

I don't have time for this stuff!

The first time we try a new activity it is awkward. Think about an instance from your own life experiences. It might have been learning to play an instrument, speak a foreign language, or master a new job. With practice, the process became habit, a "natural" part of you. The same holds true with goal setting. Once you learn the art of goal setting, you will be well on your way to achieving your desires. Goal setting is all about setting your sights on something you wish to achieve or change. You then make a plan—and move toward that result.

But, first, you must know what is in your control to fix or change. Activity 3.1 will help you make this determination.

FIX WHAT?

Let's say you wish to do better in math class. What's the first thing you have to do? You must first understand why you are not doing well. That is, before you can fix the problem, you have to know what you are fixing.

For this activity, pick a class (or something in your life outside of school that needs fixing). Write this on the line below:

I need to fix/change _____ .

Now briefly explain why you need to change this: _____

_____

_____

_____

Here comes the tricky part. From the following list, choose the items that are the biggest challenges for you with this problem. Check as many as apply; then at the end briefly explain why.

○ Teacher

○ Parent

○ Student

○ Friend

○ School administration

○ Government

○ Boss

○ Society

○ Other (specify) _____

○ Some combination (specify) _____

_____

_____

_____

Look at what you have checked. What is *your* connection to each? Can you, in fact, make an immediate impact on each one you checked? Or are some more long term and therefore not of help to you right now? For instance, you may believe you are doing poorly in math because the government requires all students to take so much math in order to move through school. Well, that may be the case. But you probably aren't going to change the government by the time the semester ends!

The point: Pick what you can have an impact on, and then go after it.

SUCCESS
STRATEGY

You must be able to make realistic assessments of what is within your ability to change—and what is not. Too often, we attempt to fix what we cannot, should not, or will not. First, identify the *what* and the *why*. Make a realistic assessment of *where* to go and *what* steps to take. Here are four simple questions to ask yourself:

- *What* happened?
- *Why* did it happen?
- *Where* do I go from here?
- *What* is my first step? (My second step?)

"Meaningful specific" or "wandering generality": Goals provide direction

Goals provide focused direction. That is, they allow us to pick the *what*. If you do not know where you are headed, it is very difficult to reach your destination.

Zig Ziglar has been on the lecture circuit for decades as the acknowledged guru of motivational thinking. He reminds his audiences of the need to be goal directed. Ziglar emphasizes that people without well-written and well-attended goals wander like lost sheep. He urges each audience member to evaluate whether or not he or she is a "meaningful specific or a wandering generality."[1] In other words, do you have direction or not?

What does a clearly stated goal look like?[2]

SUCCESS
STRATEGY

A clear goal is *written*. Once in writing, it becomes an affirmation of intent. Put it where you will see it every day. You cannot—and do not want to—ignore this important challenge you have established. Some people find the process of actually "writing" a goal awkward and a waste of time. Nevertheless, this is a valuable exercise as you develop the habit of establishing long-range plans. So sharpen that pencil and get ready to write.

A clear goal must be *specific*. Exactly what do you wish to accomplish? Saying "I want to raise my English grade" is admirable, but it lacks specificity. How much do you wish to raise it? By when? How will you know when you achieve the goal? In other words, be specific and measurable.

"I want to get a B in my English class by the end of the semester" is a much clearer statement of your desire. There is no doubt as to what you wish to accomplish. You have also identified when you wish to accomplish the goal.

A clear goal has to be *realistic*. It should be challenging, yet attainable. The deadline also must be "doable." Saying you will raise your English grade from an F to an A by the end of the week is not realistic. Challenge, but do not frustrate, yourself. I have seen students try to turn around an abysmal term, only to become discouraged because they set their sights unrealistically high. The sky (ability level) may indeed be the limit, but make sure you know exactly where *your* sky is. My sky is different from yours. Set high goals—but make sure they are realistic.

A clear goal must have a *road map*. Know where you are going, how you are going to get there, and when you plan on arriving. Otherwise you are aim-

---

[1]Zig Ziglar, *How to Get What You Want* (New York: Simon & Schuster, 1978), audiocassette.

[2]For a more detailed discussion, refer to Susan B. Wilson, *Goal Setting* (New York: American Management Association, 1994), 4–9.

Climbing the "mountain of success."

exhibit 3.1

Long range: What do you want?

Midrange: Steps to long range

Short range: Steps to midrange

less, clueless, and wasting your time. Simplify the goal into manageable and bite-size steps. Once you have a long-range goal, you will need some short- and midrange steps to achieve it. Look at Exhibit 3.1. Visualize your goal at the top of the triangle. What steps will you take to get there? Take your time in choosing these steps. You want to *motivate,* not overwhelm, yourself.

Here is an example of a "road map":

Long range:
- Attain an A in math by the end of the semester.

Midrange:
- Complete all assigned homework.
- Correct and rework any problems marked as incorrect on homework or tests.
- See the instructor at least once per week for extra help. This may be for remediation or a chance to work additional problems.
- Find a study group (if this fits your learning style).
- Participate in class.
- Get As on all the tests.

Short range:
- Get the class textbook(s).
- Review the introduction and table of contents of the textbook(s).
- Carefully read the instructor's course description, assignment page, and any other handout.

A clear goal anticipates the "glitch factor." As Murphy's Law states, if something can go wrong, it probably will. Your goals will not be immune to this universal "law." Don't become paranoid, but do try to anticipate some of the problems you may encounter along the way. By doing so, you will be prepared to meet the challenge of any obstacle and will not feel demoralized.

A clear goal has built-in incentives. Even though you want to reach a point where your goals are intrinsically motivating, it's a good idea to recognize your achievements. Provide appropriate rewards as you make progress. In fact, establish a schedule of incentives (rewards) that coincide with the "bite-size steps" mentioned earlier, such as the following:

Long range:
- Attain an A in math by the end of the semester.
  Incentive: Take your well-deserved "long weekend" of rest and relaxation.

Midrange:
- Complete all assigned homework.
  Incentive: Once you have accomplished this each week, treat yourself to a movie or a special dinner.
- Correct and rework any problems marked as incorrect on homework or tests.
  Incentive: Get that new CD or book you've been wanting.
- See the instructor at least once per week for extra help. This may be for remediation or a chance to work additional problems.
  Incentive: Get a pizza with a friend.
- Find a study group (if this fits your learning style).
  Incentive: After each meeting, go to the student center and visit with friends.
- Participate in class.
  Incentive: At the end of each week, make plans for a special "getaway" weekend at the end of the semester.
- Get As on all the tests.
  Incentive: After each A, plan a "fun" evening activity.

Short range:
- Get the class book(s).
  Incentive: Treat yourself to a soda.
- Review the introduction and table of contents of the textbook(s).
  Incentive: You're already ahead of the game. Relax and enjoy the first day of class.
- Carefully read the instructor's course description, assignment page, and any other handout.
  Incentive: Go for a leisurely walk around campus.

Now go to Activity 3.2 and do the same thing for a personal goal.

W.I.N.: Do you know what's important now?

Successful athletic coaches motivate their student athletes. When their players confront a difficult choice, coaches oftentimes instruct them to follow the principle of W.I.N.—<u>W</u>hat's <u>I</u>mportant <u>N</u>ow.

Every day, no matter how small or seemingly insignificant, take some step toward your goal. Ask yourself, "What's important now for me to achieve my goal?" Once you have identified the step, act on it. If you do not make progress toward your goal, no one else will.

Okay. Let's put this information to work. Take a moment now to work on "Buddy's Goals" in Activity 3.3.

YOUR PERSONAL ROAD MAP TO ACHIEVING YOUR GOAL   ACTIVITY 3.2

Fill in the following "road map" for a personal goal and provide incentives for
each of the steps.

LONG RANGE:

_____

_____

_____

_____

_____

_____

_____

MIDRANGE:

_____

_____

_____

_____

_____

_____

_____

_____

SHORT RANGE:

_____

_____

_____

_____

_____

_____

_____

_____

ACTIVITY 3.3   **BUDDY'S GOALS**

Your best friend has asked you to review the following list of personal goals. Put a check ("✔") in the circle next to the items you think clearly state a goal and an "x" in the circle next to the items you think are not very clear.

○ 1. I will do better in school next term.

○ 2. I will raise my math average by at least one letter grade.

○ 3. I will write something worthwhile in English class.

○ 4. I need to remember more stuff.

○ 5. I want my instructors to like me.

○ 6. I will be able to write a clear thesis statement for every essay I am assigned.

○ 7. I will study more effectively by appropriately rewarding myself each time I move closer to my goals.

○ 8. I will be nicer to my family.

○ 9. I will become a better friend.

○ 10. I will become healthier by doing at least 30 minutes of aerobic exercise four days per week.

Take a moment and jot down what is wrong with the goals you just reviewed. Pick one of the poorly written goals and make it better. Now, assume this is your goal. How are you going to be successful at achieving this goal? Briefly write your plan below.

_____

_____

_____

_____

_____

_____

_____

_____

_____

_____

_____

_____

It is obvious that Buddy's goals 1, 3, 4, 5, 8, and 9, although having worth-while intentions, do not clearly prescribe a course of action. They are just too vague. For instance, Buddy can elaborate on goal 1 so that it reads something like this:

Long range:
- I want to raise my GPA to a 3.2 by the end of the next term.

Midrange:
- I will review the notes from each class as soon after the class as possible.
- I will participate in class discussions.
- I will, when I have the choice, sit in a location with as few distractions as possible.
- I will stay up to date with all my reading assignments.
- I will not wait until the last minute to prepare for exams.

Short range:
- I will make sure I have all my "academic tools"—books, notebooks, pens, pencils, calculators, dictionary, and any other items required by my teachers. I will have these when the term begins.

Although goals 2, 6, 7, and 10 can use some clarification, they are closer to the mark because they are much more specific.

Now let's look at Activity 3.4, which will help you to put all of this information to work for you.

STEPS TO ACHIEVING YOUR GOALS   ACTIVITY **3.4**

Use the following steps to help you attain your goals:

1. Go back and look at the challenges you identified in the assessment in Activity 1.2 at the beginning of Module 1. Pick the two that provide you with the most difficulty. Write a clear goal for each. Remember to be specific and include a road map (the mid- and short-range goals).

2. Identify two personal, nonacademic desires you have. Write a clear goal for each. School is important, but it is not your whole life. Balance your activities.

3. Once you have written your specific and measurable goals, post them in a place where you will see them every day: your mirror, your computer terminal, your dresser, or the refrigerator. Look at them and remember the W.I.N. principle.

4. Work on your goals with a friend. Encourage, prod, and generally keep each other on track. Remember to look at the big picture. Imagine that you *are* successful.

Evaluate your goals: "Wanting" to do something is not the same thing as "doing" something

SUCCESS STRATEGY

Have you ever set a New Year's resolution? "I will lose 10 pounds this year." "I will go to the gym three times per week." "I will *really* buckle down and study this term." It's easy to make the resolutions—much harder to live up to them.

Set aside time—say, once a week—and evaluate your performance. You've already written your goal and road map. Look at these. What kind of progress are you making? If it is minimal, why? Is the goal realistic? Are you making a diligent effort? Maybe you need more resources.

For example, maybe you would have a better chance of getting to the gym if you had a friend go with you. Or maybe you would do better in class if you got out of that study group—which has really become a *social* group.

Be aware of any *distortion of thinking* you might experience. Because you may have encountered some glitches does not mean you are a failure. Think of the successes and build on them. Adjust your course as necessary and focus on the next step on your road map. Exhibit 3.2 may be helpful in tracking your progress.

exhibit 3.2   Tracking your progress.

GOAL	DATE OF REVIEW	PROGRESS	COMMENTS
Goal #1 Long range:			
Midrange:			
Short range:			
Goal #2 Long range:			
Midrange:			
Short range:			
Goal #3 Long range:			
Midrange:			
Short range:			

A QUICK REVIEW

As you get ready to tackle our next topic, remember that successful students

- know their challenges as well as their strengths.
- are shrewd and insightful.
- give themselves breaks and rewards.
- are proactive and can visualize success.
- are justifiably confident (each of us has a *different* sky).
- establish effective and efficient plans.
- have goals that are written, specific, measurable, realistic, valuable to them, and have an end point (or as one of my seminar participants said, "a go-to point").
- take a step, no matter how small, each day toward the desired result.
- periodically review their progress, either individually or with a friend, and revise as needed.
- have goals that fit into an overall vision of academic or personal life. In other words, successful students see their academic progress as part of a grand scheme.

Take a few moments now to review Exhibits 3.3 and 3.4.

Here are some things you can do to improve your learning environment:

- Establish a study space conducive to your needs (amount of light, temperature, and the like).
- Get a buddy to act as "support personnel"—unless your style is to work alone.

Using the information in these modules

As you read in Module 2, one size does not fit all. It will be your job to mix and match strategies to fit your particular learning style (see Exhibit 3.3). Throughout the remaining modules, you will see examples of how the auditory learner, kinesthetic learner, and visual learner can address the same topic successfully, as well as how to complement selected intelligences (see Exhibit 3.4). Finally, at the end of each module there will be reminders about the topics covered and ways that you can adjust your learning environment in order to enhance performance. Feel free to adjust as necessary. Do not take these as unquestioned absolutes, but as practical suggestions to spark further thinking on your part.

exhibit 3.3   Some possible correlations with learning styles.

TOPIC	AUDITORY	KINESTHETIC	VISUAL
Taking breaks	Listen to music.	Move about; throw a football.	Watch a video or TV.
Setting goals	Tape-record your goals and play them back.	Place your goals on a corkboard or magnetic board; move them about as priorities change.	Write the goals and post them in a conspicuous place.

exhibit 3.4   How to complement selected intelligences.

WHEN GIVEN AN ASSIGNMENT OR TASK, IF YOU ARE STRONG IN . . .	THEN ASK YOURSELF . . .
Intrapersonal intelligence/ goal setting	"How can I use my self-knowledge to help me set a goal and stick to it?"
Interpersonal intelligence/ handling criticism	"How can I use my knowledge of others to analyze the criticism that I have received?"
Linguistic intelligence/ goal setting	"How can I use my language ability to develop a clearly stated goal?"

Complete the following exercises.

1. Evaluate Bryan's quote on the first page of this module.

   _____

   _____

   _____

   _____

   _____

2. Which selection describes clear goals?

    A. written, specific, always reached

    B. written, specific, accompanied by a road map

    C. vague, open for interpretation, always focused on positives

    D. verbal/spoken only, accompanied by a road map, never reviewed until the due date.

3. What is the significance of W.I.N. as it relates to goal setting?

    A. It stresses the flexibility of goals.

    B. It shows how goal attainment is more a matter of luck than work.

    C. It indicates that goals require continual work and evaluation.

    D. It will guarantee success.

4. We process information at a certain number of words per minute. People speak at a certain number of words per minute. Which of the following is most accurate, most of the time?

    A. We process quicker than we speak.

    B. We speak quicker than we process.

    C. We process as quickly as we speak.

    D. We can't say anything definitive one way or the other.

5. Much has been said about being a "successful student." Briefly explain what this means. What criteria/standards would you establish to judge whether a student is, in fact, successful? Finally, evaluate yourself against these standards. Are you a "successful student"?

6. Why is it important to answer the question, "Fix what?"

Checklist

Checklist of Selected Tips and Strategies

As a last review, collaborate with a classmate and write a brief description of how each of the following will help you become a more successful student.

GOALS

1. Identifying learning styles

_____

_____

_____

2. Connecting between strengths and challenges

_____

_____

_____

3. Having desire

_____

_____

_____

4. Being responsible

_____

_____

_____

5. Having the right attitude

_____

_____

_____

6. Participating in active learning

_____

_____

_____

7. Practicing

_____

_____

_____

8. Connecting between competence and confidence

_____

_____

_____

9. Having incentives

_____

_____

_____

10. Establishing a plan

_____

_____

_____

11. Having written, specific, and realistic goals

_____

_____

_____

12. Being able to anticipate glitches

_____

_____

_____

13. Following the W.I.N. principle

_____

_____

_____

14. Balancing academic life and nonacademic life

_____

_____

_____

15. Periodically evaluating and adjusting your goals

_____

_____

_____

TIME MANAGEMENT

So many assignments— so little time!

"If you don't know where you are going, you'll probably end up someplace else."

—YOGI BERRA, HALL OF FAME BASEBALL PLAYER AND MANAGER

MODULE 4

Overview of This Module

GET OUT OF YOUR OWN WAY!

In the last module, you concentrated on two major points. First, you *want* to become a successful student (or a *more* successful student). Second, written goals allow you to plan and measure specific progress. Students with clear goals *empower* themselves to be responsible individuals who no longer just *react* to their environment. Each successful student needs to become an effective planner who makes efficient and effective use of time. **Goals give us a purpose.** Now let's organize time to accomplish the purpose.

Organizing time to accomplish the purpose

The major premise of this module is simple: If only you can get out of your way, you will accomplish much more.

Did you ever wonder why students feel overwhelmed and swamped? Between class work, homework, after-school activities, family responsibilities, and personal activities, there are many demands. The clock and calendar will always be there, like it or not. The key to effectively managing time is to understand what you need to accomplish and to delegate time to accomplish it. Anticipation will help to reduce pressure on you and avoid crisis. Rather than doing everything (or most things) at the last minute, let's focus on our tasks, achieve results, and have time left for ourselves. The clock keeps ticking, no matter what you do. You cannot control time. You cannot create time. But, you *can* effectively use time for your benefit.

Well-laid plans, however, can also come crashing down all around us. Have any of the following ever happened to you?

- You *knew* it would take only 30 minutes to complete that math assignment. You are now into your second hour, and you are not done yet.
- It's the night before the term paper is due. You've done all the research, written the rough draft, and you've just about completed typing at the computer. The power goes out/the printer gives you a foreign language/the hard drive crashes. You have nothing to hand in, and the teacher accepts *no excuses.*

I'm sure you could think of many more. I cannot give you a foolproof/ crisisproof time-management system, but there is one characteristic—one general strategy—*successful* students use.

Successful students are *flexible.* They can adapt to changes and unforeseen events because they have built in for the *glitch factor.* Be aware that unforeseen problems—glitches—do occur. Be prepared; anticipate a slowdown so that you can navigate around it. No matter what you have planned, try to give yourself some breathing room. This is one reason *not* to wait until the night before to complete an assignment. What if the power goes out? You won't be able to use the computer or study for an exam!

SUCCESS STRATEGY

How much study time is enough?

This is a difficult question. Since each of us has different capabilities, trying to arrive at one set amount of time for each and every student presents difficulties. But an old "formula" might provide a starting point for figuring time needs.

Years ago instructors regularly told students to budget 3 hours of study time for each hour spent in the classroom. Therefore, a three-credit class (3 hours in the classroom) required 9 hours outside of the classroom—for a total of 12 hours of commitment to one course. Whether you want to make the formula 1 for 1, 2 for 1, or 3 for 1, you need to at least think in terms of devoting time outside of class for preparation. Let's think 1 for 2: for every hour spent in the classroom plan on 2 hours outside of the class for reading, writing, research, group work, and studying for quizzes and exams. Some weeks it might be less; others it might be more. Exhibit 4.1 provides an overview of the amount of study time you should set aside based on the number of credits you are taking. This graphic representation clearly shows that the more classes you take the more demand on your time. That sounds simplistic, but many students fail to look at the big picture when planning a semester. There is a reason 12 credit hours is considered full-time by most colleges. By looking at the table in Exhibit 4.1, you can see that those 12 hours require a time commitment of 36 hours. If you are also planning on working at a job requiring 40 hours per week, then you must schedule 76 hours per week for both school and work. **That is the equivalent of two full-time jobs.** Your schedule will leave you 92 hours for everything else in your life. If you hope to get 8 hours of sleep per night (56 for the week), you now have *exhibit 4.1* Study time needed for coursework.

Number of classes you are taking this semester	Class name	Number of credits/hours in the classroom for this course	Study time (based on 2 hours for each hour in class)	Total hours per week for the course (in class *and* out of class)	Cumulative study hours for courses you are taking this term
1	English	3	6	9	9 (if you just take this 1 class)
2	Math	3	6	9	18 (for 2 classes)
3	History	3	6	9	27 (for 3 classes)
4	Humanities	3	6	9	36 (for 4 classes)
5	Biology (and lab)	4	8	12	48 (for 5 classes)

36 hours left with which to fashion a life outside of work and school. If you can do it, great! If not, stop and reevaluate before you put yourself—and your friends and family—through a nightmarish schedule. If you are exhausted by the end of the week, remember that *you* have established the schedule—not your teacher. *You* have control of how your time is spent.

Let's look at your day: Adjusting to a college schedule

Have you ever asked yourself, "Where in the world has my day gone?" Despite all of your planning, the day ends and a pile of tasks remains. This is not unusual, especially for college students. Many students enter the semester without a firm grasp on the realities of college demands. Then, usually within the first two weeks, things begin to stack up. Free time seems a luxury of the distant past. And the teacher expects work on time. What are you to do?

Well, first of all, don't blame the teacher. The teacher has a job to do and so do *you*. A better approach may be to sit down and make a list of the various transitions you are facing with college. Some relate to time, others to finances, and still others to relationships. The common denominator is that you will need to effectively address those that concern you. That is, what are you dealing with now that you didn't need to address in the past? A partial list may look like this:

- finding personal free time
- finding time to do activities with friends
- finding recreation time
- finding quality family time
- finding the time to study
- juggling work hours, school hours, and study hours
- getting enough quality sleep
- juggling family responsibilities with school expectations

Let's go a step further and complete Activity 4.1. This activity will help you become much more aware of how you use your time. How much of your time do *you* use in a productive manner? Does the picture surprise you? Do you wish to change? Well, before you can do anything about *managing* your time, you must first specifically understand how you are currently *using* time—and how you *want* to use it. Take a moment and complete Activities 4.2 and 4.3.

Are you able to identify the worthless activities or time-wasting interruptions that keep you from being as successful as you want to be? The key to being a more successful student is to focus on your challenges (refer to Module 1). The challenges in this case are those activities you listed in the first column of Activity 4.3.

True, you don't need to spend every waking minute of your day doing schoolwork. We all need diversions to stay fresh. But when those diversions interfere with your progress, you should examine them.

On a 3 × 5 index card, list your three biggest challenges when it comes to time management. (You can use the three "cards" in Exhibit 4.2; cut along the dashed line.) Use Activities 4.2–4.4 to help you focus. Now, write a goal that addresses each challenge. Put this card where it will be readily accessible, such as your wallet, pocket, backpack, or notebook. Refer to it at least once each day—and make sure you take at least one step toward that goal every day!

P³ = S: Prime Planning Principle = Simplify

SUCCESS STRATEGY

A major strategy for managing time is to look at the big picture, and then break down the overall task into smaller steps. Although the big picture is necessary in order to find our direction, it might be a bit overwhelming.

Organization expert Sarah Gilbert refers to this as the *SOS principle:* simplify, order, steps.[1] *Simplify* by breaking down things into small steps. *Order* your activities so you know what to do first, then second, and so on. Then take each *step,* one at a time, simple things first, until you reach your desired goal. Let's relate this to a classroom assignment using Activity 4.4.

[1]Sarah Gilbert, *Go for It: Get Organized* (New York: Morrow Jr. Books, 1990).

ACTIVITY 4.1 GRAPHING OUT YOUR DAY

Take a moment and draw a pie graph in the space provided. The graph shown here is only a guide. You can have as many divisions as apply to your situation, with each one representing an activity you generally do during the week. That is, in a typical week (168 hours), about how much of your time is devoted to sleeping, being in classes, doing homework, doing your job, doing chores, going to ball or dance practice, doing church-related activities, or anything else you do?

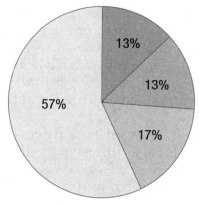

Possible categories:

Sleep	Child care duties
Meals	Church activities
Hygiene	Household chores
Class time	Recreation
Job	Homework
Practice (sports, instrument)	Other
Travel to and from school	

Use the space below to draw your graph:

PROBLEMS IN TIME MANAGEMENT[2]   ACTIVITY **4.2**

Listed below are some of the most common time-management problems facing students. Check the ones that cause you problems.

INTERRUPTIONS

- ○ Interruptions (phone calls)
- ○ Friends stopping by the house
- ○ Others requesting my help
- ○ Meetings (school, youth groups, work)

ORGANIZATION

- ○ Assignments are too big to handle
- ○ Disorganization
- ○ Attempting to do too much
- ○ Lack of planning
- ○ Procrastination (waiting until the last minute)
- ○ Too much work to do
- ○ Lack of target dates/deadlines
- ○ Too many unfinished projects/tasks—many incomplete activities
- ○ Unrealistic time estimates (expecting to finish a task in less time than it really takes)

COMMUNICATION

- ○ Unclear instructions
- ○ Not listening carefully to teacher instructions
- ○ Lack of needed information

FOCUS

- ○ Making careless mistakes so work has to be redone
- ○ Working on trivial things rather than important ones—don't prioritize well
- ○ Lack of flexibility (ability to adapt to changes)
- ○ Inability to say no when someone asks a favor

BALANCE

- ○ Lack of balance—working too much
- ○ Lack of balance—playing too much

(continued)

---

[2]Elizabeth Winstead, "Mastering Time Management" (Jacksonville, FL: Jacksonville University, no date), presentation. Adapted by permission.

EXPECTATIONS

○ Wanting my work to be perfect

○ Fearing failure

RECREATION

○ Watching too much television

○ Listening to too much music

○ Socializing

ENVIRONMENT

○ Messy study space

○ No designated study space

○ Other's mistake

FAMILY

○ My sister/brother/children

○ My parents/roommate/family

STRESS

○ Managing crises (emergency situations; urgent events)

○ Feeling stressed or overwhelmed

○ Too many different projects at the same time

○ Inability to make decisions

OTHER

○ Other: _____

_____

Review your choices. Is there one category in which most of your challenges fall? Or do you have problems in many categories? Write your reactions below.

_____

_____

_____

_____

_____

_____

WHERE DID ALL MY TIME GO?

This activity requires that you identify those items that seem to cause the *most* problems for you with your time. That is, when you run out of time, what is it that has been eating up your "pie"? What has been wasting your time?

Did you ever start an activity—a homework assignment, a household chore, a favor for a friend—but you never completed it? You had the best intentions. You really wanted to finish the project, but before you knew it, there was no time left.

Why does this happen? Chalk it up to time-wasters. You are responsible for wasting some of your time, but some time-wasters come from other sources.

Recall those times that you ran out of time and then complete the following chart.

TIME-WASTER	WHO STARTED THIS TIME-WASTER?	HOW CAN I CONTROL THIS TIME-WASTER?

(continued)

What conclusions can you draw from your responses? Write your reactions below.

_____

_____

_____

_____

_____

Now that you have identified the time-wasters, devise a plan to limit their negative effects. Here are a few solutions students have suggested:

TIME-WASTER	WHO STARTED THIS TIME-WASTER?	HOW CAN I CONTROL THIS TIME-WASTER?
1. A friend calling me on the phone	My friend	Tell my friend I'll call back after I finish my homework.
2. Watching TV	Me	Set aside time to watch TV after homework is complete; watch TV for a few minutes as a break during studies.
3. Listening to the radio/CD player	Me	Concentrate on my work; reward myself with a "music break."
4. Household chores	My parents (or roommate)	Set up a schedule.
5. Recreation	My friends and I	Don't let it interfere with what I need to accomplish. Use a schedule.
6. School!	Not me, that's for sure!	Watch it! The successful student sees school as a "positive"; there is a desire to do well. If I see school as a time-waster, I may need an attitude check and adjustment.

You might recognize some of these time-wasters or yours might be very different. What is important is that you have now recognized interruptions that are obstacles to becoming a successful student. Now it's up to you to do something about these time-wasters.

List your biggest challenges and goals to address them below.   *exhibit 4.2*

ACTIVITY 4.4   THAT INSTRUCTOR MUST THINK HOMEWORK IS ALL THERE IS TO LIFE!

Face it—homework is a fact of school life. You may not like it. It may even inter-fere with your recreational activities. It does, however, have a purpose. Homework gives you the chance to practice new skills, analyze information, and make mis-takes. Yes, *make mistakes*. This is one of the best ways to learn. Correct the errors *before* the exam and you improve your chances for better test performance.

With the right attitude and plan, you will have a better chance of making homework easier to handle. You might even learn to like it. (Well, there's always hope.) And you should still have plenty of time to pursue those per-sonal goals you have established—remember them?

Your instructor has just assigned a major project. You have to write about the accomplishments of one of the emperors of ancient Rome. The assignment is due in three weeks. Briefly jot down the steps you would take to complete the assignment—in other words, how you would manage your time in tackling this project.

DAYS 1–3:

_____

_____

_____

DAYS 4–6:

_____

_____

_____

DAYS 7–9:

_____

_____

_____

DAYS 10–12:

_____

_____

_____

DAYS 13–15:

_____

_____

_____

THAT INSTRUCTOR MUST THINK, continued   ACTIVITY **4.4**

DAYS 16–18:

_____

_____

_____

DAYS 19–21:

_____

_____

_____

A list of small steps and personally imposed deadlines might include the following:

1. Look through the textbook to narrow down a list of possible emperors. (Days 1 and 2)
2. Go to the library with this "short list" and do general research to determine which emperor to write about. (Finish by day 4)
3. Gather resource material. (By day 5)
4. Take notes. (Finish by day 9)
5. Develop an outline. (By day 10)
6. Write a first draft. (By day 13)
7. Revise and write a second draft. (By day 15)
8. Have someone proofread and comment. (By day 16)
9. Make final revisions of the draft. (By day 18)
10. Turn in on time—in fact, finish a couple of days before the deadline. This takes into account the glitch factor. (Day 19)

Your list might differ, but the important point is that you have established a flexible plan.

SUCCESS STRATEGY

Backward planning

Another strategy is to plan *backward*. Suppose you have a test scheduled in one week. Let's start with the end product—walking into class prepared for the exam. Work backward—how will you get to this point? Exhibit 4.3 provides a quick guide. Once you have established your smaller tasks, you will be ready to address the most important aspect of time management—prioritization.

exhibit 4.3   A quick guide to planning backward.

Goal: To receive an A on my science exam

DAY	TASK
Thursday, 3/13	Successfully take science exam (this is the end result).
Wednesday, 3/12	Briefly review major topics. *No* cramming necessary!
Tuesday, 3/11	Review vocabulary and potential exam questions.
Monday, 3/10	Review notes again (reread).
Sunday, 3/9	Review chapter questions in textbook. Try to identify any potential exam questions.
Saturday, 3/8	Review class notes; review vocabulary and study-guide sheets.
Friday, 3/7	Review class notes; reorganize; write a brief summary of your notes; provide a descriptive title for your notes.
Thursday (the day you started), 3/6	Make sure all textbook readings are complete.

Case Study 3

Organization

APPLYING YOUR NEW SKILLS TO THE WORKPLACE

SITUATION. Dom has just completed his first six months with a specialty advertising company. He sells pens, mugs, hats, shirts, and just about anything else on which a company can promote its logo and name. In essence, he sells "billboard space" on handheld items.

Although Dom likes his job, things have not been going well for him. He came into the position with lots of ideas and a great deal of energy. Unfortunately, he has made very few sales—many calls, but not many that resulted in cash sales.

Dom always prides himself on being quite organized but lately he seems to be moving in a cloud of dust. He moves from one thing to the next but without much direction or focus. Each day he has good intentions, works long hours, but doesn't feel like he accomplishes anything. And his desk—what a disaster! He has notes from meetings precariously sitting on one corner, business cards stuck in the top drawer, follow-up information stuck to his desk lamp with tape, and paper-clipped items throughout his calendar. Needless to say, he is forever losing things.

After a Monday morning staff meeting, Dom approaches one of the veteran sales representatives.

"Juanita. Do you have a moment to talk sometime today?"

"Sure," says Juanita. She looks at her planning calendar. "How about 4:30. I'll be done with my cold calls and planning for tomorrow's calls. Why don't you stop by my desk then?"

YOUR PROPOSED SOLUTION. What do you see as Dom's major problem? How would you approach the solution? Can you propose at least three alternative solutions?

PROPOSED SOLUTION. Dom stops by Juanita's office later that afternoon. He is not in a panic about the situation but he is concerned. He realizes it's time to stop and look at what is and is not working.

Stop. Dom explains the situation to Juanita. She asks to see his planner. He excuses himself, goes around the corner to his office, returns with a fistful of notes, and plops them on Juanita's desk.

"Where is your planner?" she asks.

"I never had any luck with those things," replies Dom. "I find I can see better what I have to do if I can spread out my notes in front of me."

"How about your notes from the sales meetings? Where are they?" Juanita says while pushing her hand through the impossible stack of notes in search of something familiar.

Dom excuses himself once again and returns momentarily with a three-inch-thick pocket folder with paper sticking out of it at all angles.

Juanita looks at the papers scattered before her, shakes her head in disbelief, and then looks at Dom. "Do you know what your problem is?"

"Yeah," replies Dom, "I'm not making any sales!"

"That's a symptom. The problem is your organization."

"You mean *lack* of organization," he sighs.

Alternatives.   Juanita gets up from her desk and goes to the chalkboard on the other side of her office that she uses for tracking her sales.

"You've got three alternatives, as I see it." She picks up a piece of chalk and starts listing them.

"First, you can find a job that doesn't require you to map out your own day. Find one that pretty much structures your day from start to finish. Someone else will plan what you have to do.

"Second, you can stay here and continue as you are.

"Or, third, you can stay here and get involved in one of the organizational skills workshops the company budgets for its employees. You received information on this in your employee orientation packet."

Consequences.   "Now, let's evaluate each of the choices," says Juanita. "I want you to tell me what you think of each one."

"I can tell you I don't like option number 1," says Dom, as he points toward the chalkboard. "I love this place. I don't want to find another job, though it has crossed my mind."

"I don't think you should leave either," agrees Juanita. "You're struggling now, but you have a talent for this business. We just need to get you focused."

Dom continues with his evaluation. "As for option number 2, I sure as blazes can't continue doing the same stuff. What is that old saying? 'If you keep doing what you're doing, you'll keep getting what you're getting.'"

Juanita smiles. "Great! That brings us to number 3."

"I read about that workshop, but do I really need a daylong session on how to use a calendar," protests Dom.

"Oh, it's much more than that," counters Juanita. "For instance, when do you make your calls to perspective clients? When do you block out time for your follow-up calls? When do you schedule your on-site visits? When do you do your reports? Is there a time you set aside to read the latest information about our business and our competitors?"

Dom thinks for a moment. "Well, I guess I do those things at different times when I can."

Juanita peers over the top of her glasses. "Listen, Dom. You need to have a written plan just as a teacher has a lesson plan. It is critical for you to block out times for each of those activities. It pays off in productivity."

Selection.   "Guess I know what I'll be doing next week! Where do I sign up for the workshop?" asks Dom.

"Just see Cindy in human resources. She'll help you," replies Juanita.

Implementation.   Dom attends the session and immediately starts trying out the strategies. He learns how to use a day planner for a "to-do list," a weekly planner for his calls and reports, and a long-term planner to map out his goals for the quarter. He quickly learns how to organize his meeting notes, client profiles, and journal articles in a series of three-ring binders. Although he discards some strategies, he uses most of them. The result is a drastically altered approach to his workday. Within one month he sees a 10 percent increase in productivity.

Pause. "Hey, Dom, how are you doing?" asks Juanita as she pokes her head into his office.

"Great!" replies Dom. "My numbers are up, and look at my desk," he says proudly as he points to a clear and organized desktop. "I'd like to meet with you this afternoon to discuss what I've been doing and see if you have any other suggestions. Do you have time?"

"Sure do," responds Juanita. "Let's meet for a soda in the cafeteria at 4:30."

YOUR REACTION TO THE PROPOSED SOLUTION. Was this the best way for Dom to get organized? Can anyone *really* help you get organized? What about those people who seem to be hopelessly disorganized? Would this approach work for them? What would work for you as a student?

IT'S A MATTER OF PRIORITIES

What is so critical about prioritizing (establishing an order of importance)? How does this task tie in with time management?

The successful student realizes that certain tasks are more important than others. In fact, certain tasks must be completed before you can move on. A lack of prioritization will cause you to waste your time. If you start writing a research paper before you establish a rough outline, you will not have direction. The final draft will reflect this lack of direction, as will your instructor's evaluation.

Exhibit 4.4 is another handy way to keep track of your progress. Clip it, copy it for each project you have, and post it in a conspicuous place. You will want to review it regularly.

One way to set priorities is to ask yourself this question once you have established your to-do list: "If I only had time to complete one activity, what would it be? Two activities. . . ."[3] This exercise forces you to focus on the issues of importance.

SUCCESS STRATEGY

Remember to be honest with yourself and the purpose of this book. Businesspeople continually have to think of ways to use their time best. Why? Because time is money. Here is a thought to keep in mind when planning your activities. I've learned this from entrepreneurs, time-management consultants, and study skill experts: **Eighty percent of your results will come from 20 percent of your activities.**

Imagine that! Another way of looking at the same principle is that 80 percent of what we do gives us only 20 percent of our results.[4] Sounds like a lot of wasted energy. It could lead to nail biting, hair pulling, and generally a high level of stress. Learn to simplify.

If this is truly the case—and I think there is some real worth to this principle—think of the time you can save in your studies. I would make an educated guess that some students put more time into homework than is really needed. You might be better served if you reduced your expenditure of time

---

[3]Ron Fry, *How to Study* (Hawthorne, NJ: The Career Press, 1991), 84.

[4]Adam Robinson, *What Smart Students Know: Maximum Grades, Optimum Learning, Minimum Time* (New York: Crown, 1993), 81–82.

exhibit 4.4   Charting your progress.

COURSE/ INSTRUCTOR	EXAMS	TERM PROJECTS	OTHER PROJECTS
	Date: Prep needed:	Date due: Prep needed:	Specific project: Date due: Prep needed:
	Date: Prep needed:	Date due: Prep needed:	Specific project: Date due: Prep needed:
	Date: Prep needed:	Date due: Prep needed:	Specific project: Date due: Prep needed:
	Date: Prep needed:	Date due: Prep needed:	Specific project: Date due: Prep needed:
	Date: Prep needed:	Date due: Prep needed:	Specific project: Date due: Prep needed:

on schoolwork—still getting the same or better results—and left some quality time for yourselves. Whether it is 80/20, 60/40, or 50/50, the point is to shoot for effectiveness.

But what's the "trick" here? Of course, it's identifying what the important 20 percent is. It will take practice to effectively identify the pertinent material, but once you do, there will be more precious time left for things that you *really* want to devote your energies to.

Urgent vs. important: Prioritizing your activities

Dr. Stephen Covey makes a very simple yet powerful point in *The 7 Habits of Highly Effective People:* Our daily activities can be seen as either urgent (not urgent) or important (not important).[5] Those that are *urgent* cry out for immediate attention. An *important* task is one that leads us *closer to our goal(s).* (Once again, look at the goals you established in Module 3.)

Urgency and importance do not always mutually reinforce one another. As you look at the following descriptions, think of where most of your activities fall.

- If an activity is *important and urgent,* it is connected to your goals but a crisis or an immediacy is involved.

- If an activity is *not important and not urgent,* it is not connected to your goals and a crisis or an immediacy is not involved.

- If an activity is *not important but urgent,* it is not connected to your goals but a crisis or an immediacy is involved.

- If an activity is *important but not urgent,* it is connected to your goals but a crisis or an immediacy is not involved.

SUCCESS STRATEGY

The key, according to Dr. Covey, is to get as many of your activities as possible to fall into the last choice: *important but not urgent.* Urgent and not important activities tend, in many cases, to be the agenda items of other people. To manage your time effectively, you need to concentrate on those activities that move you closer to your goal—not someone else's. Do you see how this very powerful strategy easily connects with some of the strategies already introduced?

For instance, if you wait until the last minute to do an assignment *(urgent),* you are in the business of crisis management and stress production. If limited study time is frittered away by someone else *(a time-waster),* you are then concentrating on items that will not move you toward your goal *(not important).* The important tasks move you closer and closer to your goals *(W.I.N.— What's Important Now).*

SUCCESS STRATEGY

It's easy to be caught up in someone else's important activities—if *you* allow it to happen. Moreover, many times, we do not even realize this is happening. One effective strategy is to keep a diary of your activities for a week. (You may wish to glance back at the pie graph you drew earlier in this module.) Be honest with yourself. Keep a running log of *everything* you do and for how long you do it. Review it. Label the activities as *urgent* or *important.* You might be surprised at your findings. Your goal here is to fill your day with as

---

[5]Stephen Covey, *The 7 Habits of Highly Effective People* (New York: Simon & Schuster, 1989), audiocassette; Stephen Covey, A. Roger Merrill, and Rebecca R. Merrill, *First Things First* (New York: Simon & Schuster, 1994), 37.

many important activities as possible. Do what *you* need and want to do; and less of what others are demanding. In other words, act on your environment rather than react to it.

SUCCESS STRATEGY

Balance and moderation

One last note on this balancing act: recreational activities are important. Diversion and relaxation are vital—as long as they are done in moderation and do not interfere with your goals. You need to treat yourself to "downtime." Get away from the books and your study area every so often. These breaks keep you sharp, focused, and energized. Not only do you need to make a commitment to do your very best in school, but you need to promise yourself that you will maintain a balance between work and play in your life.

The costs of being out of balance can be very high, and counterproductive to what you are trying to accomplish in the classroom. Frustration, anxiety, and stress are *not* what these modules are about. Leave time in your life for you!

SUCCESS STRATEGY

Calendars

Four types of calendars are discussed next. You can use computer-generated forms or those in the more traditional book format. The point is to use some form of calendar.

This selection of calendars may raise a host of questions. What is the purpose of using four calendar formats? Do you *have* to use four calendars? When should you review your calendar? Calendars are useful, but are there any tips on how to remember to look at the calendar? Let's briefly address these and other concerns.

Long-term calendars. This particular type of calendar allows you to record and view the big picture of your grading period, semester, or school year (see Exhibit 4.5). At a glance, you are able to see which days have assignments, tests, commitments, and the like scheduled. This helps you to plan your time accordingly so that you will not be caught at the last minute doing *urgent* business. On the negative side, there is not much room to elaborate about each event or assignment.

Earlier, I mentioned the *glitch factor.* Look at your calendar; carefully examine all your due dates. As you break your big tasks into little ones, leave yourself some breathing room. If an assignment is due on the 23rd of the month, why not shoot for a completion date of the 20th? If something goes wrong, you will have given yourself at least three days in which to fix the problem, thus avoiding panic attacks and crisis management. This would be an appropriate time to use the backward-planning strategy introduced earlier.

Midrange calendars. This type of calendar provides more space to make in-depth plans (see Exhibit 4.6). The format allows you to write specific steps on the way to task completion. You can also more easily see other time constraints that you need to deal with. Once again, there isn't a great deal of writing space, but you can see the whole month's assignments and commitments at a glance.

Example of a long-term calendar.

exhibit 4.5

JANUARY

S	M	T	W	T	F	S
	1	2	3	4	5	6
7	8	9	10	11	12	13
14	15	16	17	18	19	20
21	22	23	24	25	26	27
28	29	30	31			

FEBRUARY

S	M	T	W	T	F	S
				1	2	3
4	5	6	7	8	9	10
11	12	13	14	15	16	17
18	19	20	21	22	23	24
25	26	27	28	29		

MARCH

S	M	T	W	T	F	S
					1	2
3	4	5	6	7	8	9
10	11	12	13	14	15	16
17	18	19	20	21	22	23
24 / 31	25	26	27	28	29	30

APRIL

S	M	T	W	T	F	S
	1	2	3	4	5	6
7	8	9	10	11	12	13
14	15	16	17	18	19	20
21	22	23	24	25	26	27
28	29	30				

MAY

S	M	T	W	T	F	S
			1	2	3	4
5	6	7	8	9	10	11
12	13	14	15	16	17	18
19	20	21	22	23	24	25
26	27	28	29	30	31	

JUNE

S	M	T	W	T	F	S
						1
2	3	4	5	6	7	8
9	10	11	12	13	14	15
16	17	18	19	20	21	22
23 / 30	24	25	26	27	28	29

JULY

S	M	T	W	T	F	S
	1	2	3	4	5	6
7	8	9	10	11	12	13
14	15	16	17	18	19	20
21	22	23	24	25	26	27
28	29	30	31			

AUGUST

S	M	T	W	T	F	S
				1	2	3
4	5	6	7	8	9	10
11	12	13	14	15	16	17
18	19	20	21	22	23	24
25	26	27	28	29	30	31

SEPTEMBER

S	M	T	W	T	F	S
1	2	3	4	5	6	7
8	9	10	11	12	13	14
15	16	17	18	19	20	21
22	23	24	25	26	27	28
29	30					

OCTOBER

S	M	T	W	T	F	S
		1	2	3	4	5
6	7	8	9	10	11	12
13	14	15	16	17	18	19
20	21	22	23	24	25	26
27	28	29	30	31		

NOVEMBER

S	M	T	W	T	F	S
					1	2
3	4	5	6	7	8	9
10	11	12	13	14	15	16
17	18	19	20	21	22	23
24	25	26	27	28	29	30

DECEMBER

S	M	T	W	T	F	S
1	2	3	4	5	6	7
8	9	10	11	12	13	14
15	16	17	18	19	20	21
22	23	24	25	26	27	28
29	30	31				

exhibit 4.6   Example of a midrange calendar.

			JANUARY			
SUNDAY	MONDAY	TUESDAY	WEDNESDAY	THURSDAY	FRIDAY	SATURDAY
	1	2	3	4	5	6
7	8	9	10	11	12	13
14	15	16	17	18	19	20
21	22	23	24	25	26	27
28	29	30	31			

Weekly planner and daily planner. These formats lead to the nitty-gritty of planning (see Exhibits 4.7 and 4.8). Once the week is planned, establish a to-do list and then prioritize the tasks. You can do this by time of day, urgency, or importance of the task. This is a basic building block for effective time management. You really don't need a form; a sheet of notebook paper or a spiral pad will work just as well. The point is to use something on a consistent basis.

You may wish to try a computer calendar or a digital/electronic handheld organizer. Those are fine too, but only if they match your learning and organizational style. Remember, *fancy and expensive* does not equate to *effective and efficient*.

Now, where did I put that calendar?

All the calendars in the world are useless if you don't look at them. Once you use them, it will become habit, a necessary part of your book bag. Here are some suggestions I have heard from students to help remind them to look at the calendar:

- Put the calendar at the base of your mirror, or on the dresser, or someplace you always go to each day.
- Place the calendar on the floor by your bedroom door. You'll have to walk right over it when you leave for the day.
- Write down personal activities (parties, ball games) on your academic calendar. You will be more apt to look at it if you are looking for "fun" dates.

Example of a weekly planner.   *exhibit 4.7*

	JANUARY					
S	M	T	W	T	F	S
	1	2	3	4	5	6
7	8	9	10	11	12	13
14	15	16	17	18	19	20
21	22	23	24	25	26	27
28	29	30	31			

Week of _____

Notes _____

_____

_____

_____

SUNDAY

MONDAY

TUESDAY

WEDNESDAY

THURSDAY

FRIDAY

SATURDAY

- Work with a friend. When getting used to the calendar, use the phone to call one another for a reminder to look at your calendar. Just don't let this become a time-waster.
- Get in the habit of reviewing the calendar at a regular time. For instance, be sure to look at your calendar before closing your books for the evening. It will give a last clear picture of what you need to tackle when you awaken. No surprises!
- Instill in yourself the *desire* to look at the calendar.

Whatever works for you, use it!

exhibit 4.8   Example of a daily planner.

Monday, September 6, 2004

8:00 a.m.	Review notes for history class
9:00 a.m.	History class
10:00 a.m.	Meet with biology study group (1 hour session)
11:00 a.m.	Biology lab
12:00 noon	Work out in the exercise room
1:00 p.m.	Lunch with Steve
2:00 p.m.	
3:00 p.m.	Work until 5 p.m.
4:00 p.m.	
5:00 p.m.	
6:00 p.m.	Dinner
7:00 p.m.	Study time until 9 p.m.
8:00 p.m.	
9:00 p.m.	Free time
10:00 p.m.	
11:00 p.m.	Lights out!

SUCCESS STRATEGY

How do I establish a study schedule?

When filling in your calendar for the week, why not block out time for your homework? For those who juggle family, job, extracurricular activities, and schoolwork, this might be difficult. It might even seem impossible. Here is a simple method that has worked for extremely busy students. Ask yourself the following questions and then make adjustments as necessary:

- How many courses are you taking?
- What is the approximate amount of your homework hours per course per week?

- How much of your time is already committed (class, practice, job, family, exercise, and sleep)? Look back at your pie graph in the beginning of the module.

- How much time is left for your study time?

This is a great activity to conduct *prior* to signing up for classes. You can *realistically* ascertain whether you will have time to pursue your academic and personal goals and responsibilities.

Efficiency vs. effectiveness[6]

So, armed with calendars in hand you are ready to do efficient battle with the world. Right? Maybe.

Think book bags for a moment. They allow for ease in toting textbooks, notebooks, pencils and pens, paper, a stapler, and even a hole punch. Everything in one compact area. This is efficient.

What happens, however, when you try to locate the small assignment pad or the lone piece of paper you just put in the bag? You know the pencil is at the bottom of the bag—somewhere! You have made efficient use of the bag by having all your materials close at hand, but you weren't effective.

This can happen to all of us, in or out of class. You might be doing things much faster, but you just might be going in the wrong direction. Don't let any tool, such as a calendar or book bag, become the result. Make sure it serves your purposes.

A QUICK REVIEW

Y ou've completed another topic on your journey to becoming a more successful student.

- Motivational goal setting allows you to establish a direction, course, and end point for which to aim.
- Time management provides the plan to reach the goal.

Successful students know how to

- anticipate potential obstacles.
- budget their time.
- identify what causes them time-management problems.
- develop a plan to control time-wasters.
- simplify tasks.
- establish priorities for long-, mid-, and short-range activities.
- identify and fill their week with important activities.
- establish a realistic study schedule.
- maintain a balance in their lives between academic and personal issues.

The quote by Yogi Berra at the beginning of this module is very appropriate. If you do not know where you are going, you will get lost. Life can have

---

[6]For an excellent presentation on these concepts, I recommend Covey, Merrill, and Merrill, 26.

a plan and still be adventuresome. Planning does not translate into rigidity. You can be efficient and still be spontaneous.

With this in mind, you are now ready for the classroom experience. Remember the major premise of these modules: **You want to be a successful student!**

Take a few moments now to review Exhibits 4.9 and 4.10.

---

exhibit 4.9   Summary of possible correlations with learning styles.

TOPIC	AUDITORY	KINESTHETIC	VISUAL
Using calendars	Try a handheld tape recorder.	Place priorities on index cards; physically shuffle and review cards; construct a computer-generated calendar.	Use a written calendar and notes with priorities clearly labeled; maybe draw pictures to highlight major events; use a computer-generated calendar.
Backward planning	After writing the plan, or while writing it, "talk" yourself through it.	Draw your plan.	Draw your plan or write the list.

---

exhibit 4.10   How to complement selected intelligences.

WHEN GIVEN AN ASSIGNMENT OR TASK, IF YOU ARE STRONG IN . . .	THEN ASK YOURSELF . . .
Spatial intelligence/ planning a project	"How can I use my ability to manipulate the environment to organize my time?"
Logical-mathematical intelligence/using calendars	"How can I use my ability to make order out of chaos to help me with this task?"
Linguistic intelligence/ backward planning	"How can I use my word ability to verbalize a reasonable study plan?"

Here are some things you can do to improve your learning environment:

- When scheduling your priorities, if possible, keep in mind whether you are a morning person or an evening person; schedule to meet your strengths.
- Determine whether you are more comfortable with a rigid format or a more free-form flexible format.

Complete the following exercises.

1. Evaluate Yogi Berra's opening quote found on the first page of this module.

   _____

   _____

   _____

   _____

2. The 80/20 principle refers to the idea that
   A. 80 percent of your work gives you 20 percent of your result.
   B. 80 percent of your books are useless 20 percent of the time.
   C. 80 percent of people do 20 percent of the work.
   D. 80 percent of people work only 20 percent of the time.

3. The significance of the 80/20 principle is that it
   A. is one way to focus and study more effectively.
   B. is one way to beat the system.
   C. means only 20 percent of anything an instructor says is worthwhile.
   D. is nothing more than a cute gimmick.

4. A "priority"
   A. can be different for each student.
   B. indicates an item of importance.
   C. should receive your attention.
   D. is all of the above.

5. List two advantages for each of the calendars listed below:
   Long-range calendar
   A. _____
   B. _____

   Midrange calendar
   A. _____
   B. _____

   Weekly planner
   A. _____
   B. _____

6. Your next major exam is scheduled 10 days from today. Using the strategy of backward planning, outline how you will be ready for this exam.

_____

_____

_____

_____

7. Compare and contrast "efficiency" and "effectiveness." Give an example of each.

_____

_____

_____

_____

8. Briefly describe the "glitch factor."

_____

_____

_____

_____

9. Your best friend needs your help. She always seems to have more things to do than she does time. Briefly describe three strategies you believe will help her manage this scarce resource of time.

A. _____

B. _____

C. _____

Checklist

Checklist of Selected Tips and Strategies

As a last review, collaborate with a classmate and write a brief description of
how each of the following will help you become a more successful student.

TIME MANAGEMENT

1. Being flexible

   _____

   _____

   _____

2. Graphing out the typical 168-hour week

   _____

   _____

   _____

3. Identifying problem areas

   _____

   _____

   _____

4. Identifying causes of problems

   _____

   _____

   _____

5. Identifying solutions to problems

   _____

   _____

   _____

   _____

6. Simplifying

   _____

   _____

   _____

7. Having a project time line

   _____

   _____

   _____

8. Implementing backward planning

   _____

   _____

   _____

9. Establishing priorities

10. Understanding the 80/20 principle

11. Determining urgent and important activities

12. Determining not urgent and not important activities

13. Understanding balance and moderation

14. Using long-term calendars

15. Using midterm calendars

16. Using weekly and daily calendars

17. Remembering your calendar

18. Implementing a study schedule

THE CLASSROOM EXPERIENCE

Achieving the best result

"Great minds have purposes, others have wishes."

—BENJAMIN DISRAELI,

NINETEENTH-CENTURY

BRITISH PRIME MINISTER

MODULE 5

Overview of This Module

WHAT IN THE WORLD IS THAT TEACHER DOING IN FRONT OF THE ROOM?

This section explores the classroom experience. First, we will look at the front of the room: what the teacher is doing and what the teacher's expectations are. Then we will look at the back of the room: what you are doing in class. Specifically, we will review strategies that if practiced will enable you to become a more successful student.

Teacher style and emphasis

When it comes to teaching styles, teachers come in all shapes and sizes. Think of the various teachers you have had. Their styles have ranged from lecture, to question and answer, to group work, to lab work, to discussion, to seat work. Regardless of the method of presentation, each teacher has a set of expectations for student performance. Some teachers emphasize minute details; others seek broad generalizations for application to new situations. One teacher may require you to "take ownership" of the class by being actively involved, while another instructor may require you to be a passive receptacle diligently copying his or her words of wisdom. Activity 5.1 will help you to determine just what your teachers expect from you.

IDENTIFYING WHAT YOUR INSTRUCTORS WANT FROM YOU   ACTIVITY 5.1

Here is a sampling of teacher styles and expectations. Check the ones that apply to the instructors you currently have.

I HAVE TEACHERS WHO:

- ⊙ give lecture after lecture.
- ⊙ expect students to participate in class.
- ⊙ concentrate on group work.
- ⊙ concentrate on in-class seat work.
- ⊙ are sticklers for details like dates, formulas, and classifications.
- ⊙ pay close attention to grammar and writing skills.
- ⊙ very seldom assign a writing assignment.
- ⊙ are very serious and do not allow any joking in class.
- ⊙ are very serious but do allow lighthearted moments.
- ⊙ never accept an assignment late.
- ⊙ accept assignments late, but with a penalty.
- ⊙ do not seem to care about punctuality.
- ⊙ seem to always go off on a tangent.
- ⊙ are always on target, seldom straying from the topic at hand.

If you are aware of your teachers' styles, expectations, and emphases, you are on the way to improved performance. Preparation for the class is more focused and anxiety should lessen. For those of you who are able to choose your own teachers, knowledge of teacher methodology is a vital factor in determining your schedule—or at least it is for the successful student.

Identification of teacher style + expectations = classroom success

Clip and copy the chart in Activity 5.2. Complete it and place it at your home study area so you will always be reminded of these important expectations. Be sure to complete one for each class you have.

ACTIVITY 5.2   WHAT DOES MY TEACHER EXPECT FROM ME?

Course title:

Teacher:

Requirements of the course:

- ○ Maintain a notebook.
- ○ Complete mostly reading homework.
- ○ Complete mostly writing homework.
- ○ Complete both reading and writing homework.
- ○ Participate in class.
- ○ Do group work.
- ○ Other.

My teacher will grade me with

- ○ Reading quizzes.
- ○ Homework assignments.
- ○ Class participation.
- ○ Exams.
- ○ Projects.
- ○ Research papers.
- ○ Group work.
- ○ Other.

My teacher conducts the class by primarily doing

- ○ Group work.
- ○ Lecture.
- ○ Lots of class discussion.
- ○ Worksheets.
- ○ In-class problems or writing assignments.
- ○ Work out of the textbook.
- ○ Other.

My teacher's tests for this course are primarily

- ○ Multiple choice.
- ○ Matching.
- ○ Completion/fill in the blank.

- ○ True/false.
- ○ Short answer.
- ○ Essay.
- ○ Some combination of the above.
- ○ Other.

My biggest challenge/weakness in this class is

- ○ Taking notes.
- ○ Understanding the teacher.
- ○ Dealing with distractions.
- ○ Staying focused.
- ○ Completing my homework on time.
- ○ Following instructions.
- ○ Answering questions orally.
- ○ Working with groups.
- ○ Getting ready for tests.
- ○ Dealing with the volume of homework.
- ○ Being a procrastinator.
- ○ Managing my time.
- ○ Getting to class on time.
- ○ Having excessive absences.
- ○ Having a negative attitude.
- ○ Feeling hungry.
- ○ Feeling sleepy.
- ○ Other.

Steps I can take to do better in this class:

- ○ Seek tutoring from the teacher.
- ○ Seek tutoring from a classmate.
- ○ Seek help from my parents.
- ○ Follow through on my assignments.
- ○ Reevaluate how I budget my time.
- ○ Ask for a seat change.
- ○ Review my notes on a more regular basis than I already do.

(continued)

○ Prepare earlier for exams.

○ Break big projects into smaller, easier-to-manage steps.

○ Be on time for class.

○ Be absent less often.

○ Ask the teacher if there are any practice tests.

○ Seek computer-assisted instruction where available.

○ Read the textbook more carefully.

○ Review class notes regularly.

○ Devote more time to quality studying.

○ Other.

SUCCESS STRATEGY

Now take a moment to complete the chart in Activity 5.3. This is not an evaluation of your teachers but, rather, another reflective awareness activity for you. (Refer to the checklist in Activity 5.2 to help you with columns three and four.)

Look at the style and emphasis columns. Now look at your behavior. Are there any connections or relationships? Do you seem to be more on task in certain classes than others? If so, why? In which classes, if any, do you have the most difficulty staying on task?

If you have been honest in completing the activity, the information will provide graphic proof of how teacher method ties in directly with student distractibility and performance. It's obvious that certain classes require more focused energy from you. This also says something about your individual learning style; that is, how you learn best. (Refer to Module 2.) You can use this information when choosing instructors for the next semester.

DOES INSTRUCTOR BEHAVIOR AFFECT MY BEHAVIOR?

COURSE TITLE	INSTRUCTOR	INSTRUCTOR'S STYLE (LECTURE, GROUPS, DISCUSSION, LABS, OTHER)	INSTRUCTOR'S EMPHASIS (DETAILS, THEORIES, DATES, GENERALIZATIONS)	YOUR BEHAVIOR (SKIP CLASS, SLEEP, PAY ATTENTION, LISTEN ATTENTIVELY)

SUCCESS STRATEGY

Now let's look at some difficult situations and what you can do to turn them into successful classroom experiences. Remember, the teacher is in control of the room. You cannot control the teacher, but you *can* control the manner in which you respond, which may in turn have an effect on how the teacher responds to you.

For example, the teacher is boring, mean-spirited, and a difficult grader. If there is a personality clash with this particular instructor, sit back and evaluate the situation. (You can use the SAC-SIP problem-solving method here; see Module 1.) Have you contributed to the problem? What can you do to change the predicament? A common approach is to transfer to another class. While this may be appropriate in some instances, it tends to be an easy way out that masks deeper challenges. Is the instructor a difficult grader, or is it simply that you lack some basic process skills? Be honest. *Just because you got an A in the previous course does not mean you were challenged.* Maybe this is the time to work a little harder and learn those skills you will need now and in the future. (I never said it would be easy!)

In another class, the teacher seems to assign only "busy work." Remember, effective teachers give homework with a purpose. You may not see the purpose, but that doesn't mean one doesn't exist! This means doing your reading assignments. Not having to "turn in" an assignment doesn't mean it's not homework. The first step to effective studying is to complete your daily assignments. Studying requires ongoing review, diligence, and preparedness.

- Even if you have no specific assignment, review your class notes and activities nightly. You will know where you have been and where you are going the next day. Just because there isn't a *new* assignment it doesn't mean you don't have homework.

- Although it sounds very elementary, have all your "tools." An athlete wouldn't think of going to baseball practice without a mitt or spikes. A band member doesn't show up for a performance without the proper instrument. Why, then, walk into class without a pen, pencil, paper, or whatever else the instructor expects?

  - Bring a good attitude. Athletes prepare themselves mentally for a game. Dancers and musicians ready themselves for a performance. Think of each class as a contest or opening night. Be ready for it. Don't strike out; don't forget your lines. Remember, one of the characteristics of a successful student is the *desire* to do well.

    Of course, distractions do occur. We cannot always be focused—though that is one of our goals. But if we continually "drift" from class, some adjustments need to be made.

I really want to pay attention in class . . . but it's not easy

The class has just started. You're in your seat, the teacher starts the lesson, and you start to "drift away." You really want to pay attention, but it is so difficult. Take a few minutes now to complete Activity 5.4, another reflective self-assessment activity.

WHAT CAN YOU DO TO FIGHT DISTRACTIONS?   ACTIVITY 5.4

First, let's identify some reasons that you might start to daydream or become restless.

- ○ The student next to you is making noise.
- ○ The teacher is boring.
- ○ There is noise right outside the classroom window.
- ○ You are hungry.
- ○ You stayed up late last night to watch a movie.
- ○ You are reading a note from your friend.
- ○ You are writing a note to your friend.
- ○ You do not understand the lesson.
- ○ You have left all your class material (pencils, pens, paper, book) at home or in the car.
- ○ You are thinking about the coming weekend.
- ○ You do not know the answer to any of the questions the teacher is asking the class.
- ○ You are attracted to the student sitting next to you.
- ○ A great sporting event is scheduled for after school.
- ○ It is the last class of the day.

Now that you have identified the distractions, what can be done to control them? List your methods to overcome these distractions. Keep in mind your learning style. Maybe the reason you have been distracted is that you are working against your individual and unique needs as a student. Work with a classmate to brainstorm additional strategies.

_____

_____

_____

_____

_____

_____

_____

_____

SUCCESS STRATEGY

One overriding strategy helps to fight off classroom distractions: *concentration.* Always remember your purpose. Look for verbal and nonverbal clues by your teacher. Be an active participant—ask questions. By reviewing your notes and activities nightly, you can arrive at *your own* questions that relate to the material. Can you determine what the big picture is? What point is the teacher trying to make? Listen to your classmates' questions and answers; they can have many interesting insights. Take good notes and then review those notes.

You can also make distractions work *for* you. Allow yourself the luxury of accepting the distraction. Distracting thoughts can be merciless, continually nagging and interrupting. Once that thought intrudes, welcome it in. Say to yourself, "This is not the best time for me to deal with this distraction, but I'll listen for a moment." If possible, jot down the distraction on a piece of paper: "Call Joey tonight"; "When do the Yankees play next?"; "Gee, I'm bored with school!" Now, let go. You have mentally told yourself that you will address the issue later.[1]

Finally, there will be times when you will have boring and opinionated instructors. Resist the temptation to judge. Actively engage the lesson. Evaluate the instructor and his or her message later. Remember, boredom is not an acceptable excuse to "check out."

WHAT IN THE WORLD AM I DOING IN THE BACK OF THE ROOM?

A word about being "cool"

Visualize yourself as a teacher. You are in your classroom looking out at a room full of students. And every student *behaves just as you do* in class. Each student responds, acts, and writes as you do. Are you pleased with this picture? Be honest.

When a student responds to a teacher request with rude and inappropriate comments, there are a few points the student is telegraphing to the teacher:

- I am not a successful student.
- I am so insecure about my knowledge in this class that I have to act this way to protect myself.
- I have no respect for the teacher.
- I am *not* cool!

You see, if you are *cool* you don't have to make a point of showing it. Those who try to *show* they are cool just aren't. Not only are they not cool, but they also have placed themselves in a terrible position with the teacher. Remember that teachers are individuals with feelings and emotions just like students. If you continually try to make them look bad, you are the one who probably will lose. Trust me on this one.

SUCCESS STRATEGY

Creating a positive classroom experience

The teacher is the professional responsible for developing a learning environment that is inviting and productive. But you are also important in this process. If you watch the successful students in your classes, I'm sure you will see the following characteristics:

---

[1]Also see Dave Ellis, *Becoming a Master Student,* 7th ed. (Boston: Houghton Mifflin, 1994), 139; and Walter Pauk, *How to Study in College,* 5th ed. (Boston: Houghton Mifflin, 1993), 65–66.

- They are punctual for class.
- They do not continually watch the clock. You can't, no matter how much you want to, make those hands move any faster. You can't control or create time, nor can you make it go any faster.
- They are actively involved in class activities.
- They do not sleep in the back of the room or pass notes to a friend.
- They do not do homework for one class in another class.
- They ask appropriate questions.
- They realize an absence does not excuse them from the responsibility of doing work they missed.
- They have an up-to-date assignment pad to keep track of all homework, projects, and exam dates. No surprises here.
- They always (or most always) come to class prepared and ready to work.
- They do not start packing up their books before the class is over. The old saying still pertains: "The clock does not dismiss the student; the teacher does." Packing up early means you might miss an assignment or a last important point. At the very least, it's definitely rude.

By adopting these traits, you will turn your classroom experience into a positive and successful one.

Active learning

SUCCESS STRATEGY

You want to be an active learner in class. What does that mean? The key to success in the classroom is participation. Sit as close to the front of the room as possible. You want to have a "ringside seat" for questions, answers, and the general presentation. If you can discuss a concept, you have a much better chance of understanding it. If your teacher's style does not lend itself to class discussion, you can still be actively involved by anticipating the teacher's lecture, asking questions of yourself, and the like. But you need to remain focused. Easy? No. Beneficial? You bet! Remember the 80/20 principle (see Module 4)? If you understand the big picture, the teacher's style, and the teacher's expectations, you will know what the important material is. If you understand the major points, you will not need to write every word said by the instructor. The more notes you take, the more you have to wade through to get ready for an exam.

Is your notebook open, pen ready, and mind receptive?

One student task is to take notes on the important material. What strategies can you use to sharpen your note-taking skills?

- You can turn to an educational TV channel and take notes on the evening's presentation. Have a friend do the same thing and then compare notes.
- If you would rather work alone, videotape the same presentation. Take notes at the same time you are taping the presentation. Then replay the presentation and compare your notes to the taped material. Did you miss anything?
- You could also tape-record a teacher lecture, take notes, and replay the tape later. As a rule, I do not recommend taping teacher presentations. Students

end up taping each lesson but fail to take notes at the same time. This type of taping ignores the real issue—improving note taking. Practice is necessary. I also have found very few students ever listen to the tape again. For this one activity, however, I do relent. If used, taping should only be a stopgap measure until you are more comfortable with your note-taking skills. (Make sure you always get teacher permission before taping a presentation.)

After following one of these strategies, look at the notes you wrote. How did you know what to write? How did you know what was important?

SUCCESS STRATEGY

Note-taking styles

Note taking is a very personal activity. You have to organize your notes in a format that complements your learning style. We next discuss three very general styles. You may not find any of these particularly appealing. That's okay, but find a style that works for you and be consistent in its use.

The following examples of the three general styles of note taking look at the goals of labor, management, and the government in our economic system. The topic here is not the important point. It could just as easily have been the success of the Beatles or the reactions in the Krebs cycle. What you want to examine is *how* you take notes.

If you learn best by using very structured and orderly models, the format in Exhibit 5.1 may be for you. Note that this outline is organized with Roman

exhibit 5.1   Note taking: The traditional outline.

> I. What do the players in our economy want?[2]
>   A. Management
>   1. profit
>   2. efficiency
>   3. order
>   B. Labor
>   1. increased wages
>   2. safe working conditions
>   3. adequate benefits
>   C. Government
>   1. business expansion
>   2. low unemployment
>   3. order

[2]See Steve Piscitelli, *Does Anyone Understand This Stuff? A Student Guide to Organizing United States History* (Atlantic Beach, FL: Author, 2001), 88.

numerals, capital letters, and Arabic numerals (lowercase letters would be used for a fourth classification). Each indentation represents a smaller classification (or information of lesser importance).

Perhaps your learning style does not allow you to easily use this note-taking strategy. You are not too sure where the instructor is moving with the lecture, and it is extremely difficult to determine what a subcategory of a larger category is. In other words, you need a model that allows more flexibility.

Note that the model in Exhibit 5.2 has the same basic information. If your learning style is such that pictures help you learn, why not put your notes in a picture-like (or graphlike) structure? It is also very easy to add information when using this model; a simple arrow or line can be used.

The format in Exhibit 5.3 is an adaptation of the Cornell Note-Taking System.[3] Note that there is an expanded margin on the left side of the page for student questions or other organizing comments to use as a study guide. This model is more linear in fashion than the preceding model, yet not quite as structured as the first model.

Preferred organizing methods vary among students. No doubt there are countless others. See Exhibit 5.4 for yet one more.

Note-taking strategies: Cluster or flow-chart notes.[4]   *exhibit 5.2*

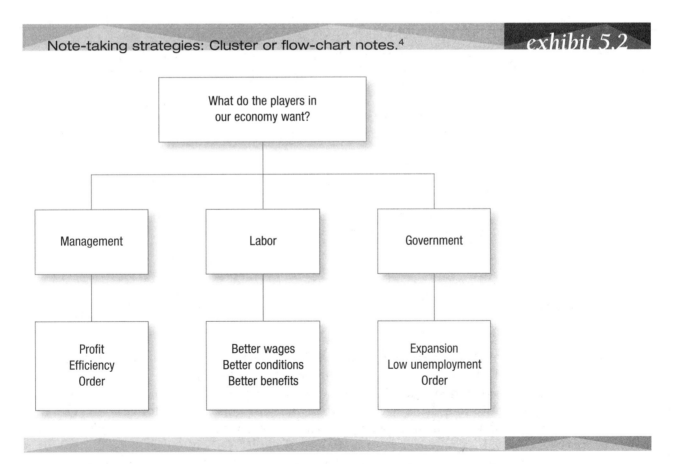

[3]Pauk, 110–14. Also see Nancy L. Matte and Susan H. G. Henderson, *Success Your Style! Right- and Left-Brain Techniques for Learning* (Belmont, CA: Wadsworth, 1995), 78–82.

[4]Various labels have referred to this style of notes. Some people call it mapping; others, such as Matte and Henderson, use the term *spidergram*.

exhibit 5.3   Note taking: Side-by-side notes.

Personal Study Guide (developed after class when reviewing your notes)	Date: Class Notes
Who makes up management? How can profits be increased?	What do the players in our economy want? Management wants: Profit, efficiency, order
Who represents labor? What methods can labor use to achieve its goals?	Labor wants: Wages, conditions, benefits
Why is government concerned about labor and management?	Government wants: Expanding economy, low unemployment, order
What is an example of an expanding economy? What goals do the three players share? How are the three players different?	

The format[5] in Exhibit 5.4 allows you to arrange the *intricate parts* around the body of an *issue*. Even if you cannot take class notes in this manner, this format allows quick organization. It can be helpful in reorganizing your notes prior to a test, as well as putting your thoughts together for an essay. This type of model might be what you need to jog your memory. Take a look at Exhibit 5.5 for an example of a completed model. As with all models, this is only a guide. You may have other items listed. Use these notes to brainstorm other events. The idea is to generate ideas, relationships, and analysis.

---

[5]Some people refer to this type of overview as spidergrams while others call it clustering. For an example of this method, see Matte and Henderson, 84.

Diagram of a spidergram.

exhibit 5.4

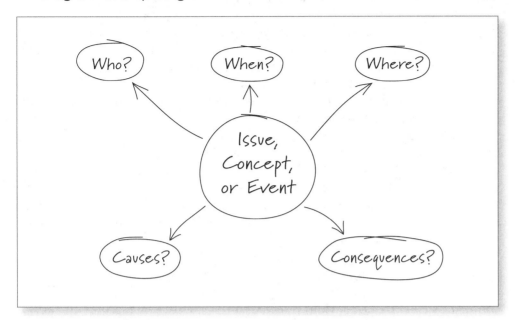

Example of a completed spidergram.

exhibit 5.5

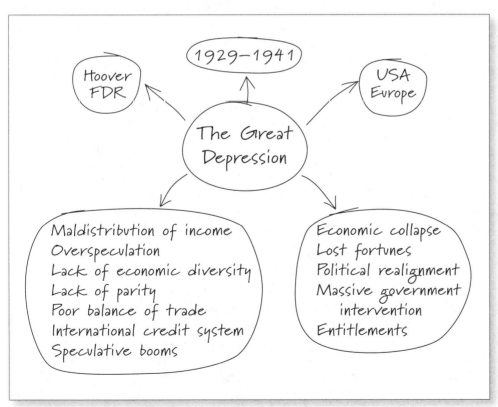

Once again, the note-taking style you choose is really a personal thing. No one can tell you which one to use. Pick one that fits your own learning style, and consistently use it. For instance, if you are a very *organized and linear* thinker, the *traditional outline* might work best for you. It is structured, so you can easily see what comes first, second, and so on. If you tend to be more of a *free-form or picture* thinker, more creative and less bound to structure, something like the *flow-chart notes* might be more fitting.

Do not feel that you must copy a note-taking style exactly as shown. Remember, you can easily revise these styles to come up with your very own. That is, pick and choose those parts of each style with which you are comfortable. Examine the notes you take in class now. Do they resemble one of the styles we have examined? Maybe you have a totally different style. That is okay as long as it works! Are your notes organized? If so, great! If not, develop one. *Organized class notes will help you focus* on teacher expectations and emphasis. Even if a class is "easy" and you feel notes are not needed, take them anyway. You need the practice.

One final comment. Look at the side-by-side notes outline. This style, as indicated, provides space for a student-developed study guide. You can do this with any style you decide to follow. By preparing a study guide, you are developing possible test questions. In essence, you are actively engaged in organizing the information, while also getting ready for the next test (see Module 9).

SUCCESS STRATEGY

Now that you have your notes, what should you do next? Applying the 3Rs

Taking clear notes in class is another step closer to becoming a successful student—but there is still more to do. Studying truly begins the next time you look at your notes. When should that be? It should be as soon as possible after the class. Three strategies—the 3Rs (review, relate, reorganize)—will help you understand the material and cut down on last-minute test preparation.

Review. Look at the class notes you wrote earlier in the day. Is there anything that is not clear? Do you understand all principles, generalizations, and theories? If you have questions, put an asterisk or question mark in the margin of your notes. Be sure to ask these questions at the beginning of the next class session. If you wait until the night before the unit exam, it will be rather difficult to get a clarification from the teacher. In addition, by asking the question in class, you are actively participating—another one of our strategies. This is one of the *important* activities you need to do each evening.

Relate. Too many times, students attempt to memorize isolated pieces of information. This is a daunting and boring task. As an alternative, look at previous notes and reading assignments. Are there any connections? Do you see emerging trends or patterns? Once you start seeing this big picture, the material will make sense and be easier to remember.

For example, let's look at the previous sample notes on the players in the economy. You would want to compare these notes to your textbook assignment. Is there a section on labor? What does it present? Are there subsections in the text about wages and conditions of employment? Can you fill in your notes with any of the information from the textbook? Do this with each section of the notes.

Similar situations appear in the workforce. Perhaps you have attended a seminar on a new product you will be selling. How does the new product fit in with other products in your line? Can you show a client how this innovation will connect with other products you have sold?

Reorganize. As you look over your notes, see if there is a clearer way in which to see the big picture. Sometimes an instructor will present material out of order, or go off on tangents. Reshuffle your notes so they make sense to *you*. You may wish to write a brief outline in the margin of the notes (similar to what you find at the beginning of each chapter in this book). I ask my students to come up with their own title for the day's class. If they can do this, they understand the big picture.

Continue to reorganize and relate each night in this manner. By test time, you should have only one or two pages of notes. No more cramming for the exam. What you have developed is an ongoing study guide. *Note taking is a vital part of test preparation.*

One of my enterprising students used to take her class notes in various colored pens. She had developed her own system of each color representing a certain level or importance of information. I have to admit that watching her with a fistful of pens, switching from pen to pen as I went from point to point, was one of the most unorthodox strategies I have witnessed. It did, however, work for her. It not only helped with initial organization, but also with reorganization later. Remember, choose those techniques that best fit your style. (As a side note, this student is now a successful dentist.)

Okay . . . but I still don't get the big picture

Even the best note taker can be overwhelmed by a mountain of information and miss the big picture. Use the following strategies in conjunction with the 3Rs.

SUCCESS STRATEGY

Title/Summary/Details (TSDs). Students have a better chance of understanding class notes if they can put the material into their own words. Copying verbatim notes from the board or PowerPoint presentations will not be useful if you cannot explain the material in your language. Here is a simple activity you can practice when reviewing each day's class work.

Start by giving the notes a title, followed by a one- or two-sentence summary. Then list approximately three facts that would support your summary. (This will be a great base on which to build the writing skills we will discuss in Module 7.)

Using the sample lecture in Activity 5.5, you might develop the following TSDs:

T: (What is the big picture? What title effectively captures the day's notes?) What is the best teaching style?

S: (How would you summarize the notes in a sentence or two?) Although no one can tell me how to teach, there are a few basic methods I should use on a regular basis to hold the interest of my students.

Ds: (What do you see as the major details in the lecture? What questions might the instructor pose on the exam?) Instructor centered teaching; content centered teaching; student centered teaching.

Keep your TSDs at the beginning of your unit material. Add to them each day. When test time rolls around, you will have a practical study guide from which to review.

If TSDs do not help you, try working backward. First, identify the major facts of the lecture; second, the major issues; third, the big picture. Finally, *try* to write a thesis statement about the material. Capture the essence of the lecture.

ACTIVITY 5.5 DEVELOPING TSDs

Here are some sample teacher notes from an Introduction to Education class on the topic of the characteristics of an effective teacher. After reading these notes, circle the major facts of the lecture, and then underline any major issues. Finally, write a statement that effectively underscores the main point of the presentation.

> I can't tell you how to be an effective teacher. Hopefully, I have modeled some activities or behaviors that you will want to duplicate in your classroom. There is no one way to teach. We all have to adopt different approaches to fit our personalities. As long as you remain the student's foremost advocate, you should do well.
>
> Here are a few styles. You have seen them all, I'm sure, from time to time.
>
> Instructor centered: The teacher is the imparter of knowledge; he is the model for the students to follow. The emotionally exciting educator will keep students on the edge of their seats. The emotionally sterile teacher will keep students on the edge of their sleep!
>
> Content centered: This type of teacher believes the content is the end all and be all of education. Instruction is determined by the text, subject matter, and curriculum.
>
> Student centered: The role of the teacher is that of facilitator. Developing inferential abilities in the students is considered vital. The teacher will use inquiry, discovery discussion, simulations, values clarification, brainstorming, and independent study. Learning contracts may be an integral part of this approach.
>
> The best style? Keep one thing in mind: VARIETY. Try to vary your teaching style from day to day—even within one class period. This will help the students—and you. Your elementary school teachers know what I am saying better than anyone else.
>
> Classroom observations: Look around your school. Who is doing what? Visit classrooms. Talk to the master teachers. You'll know who they are. Be big and accept the fact that you can learn from a colleague.

Perhaps you identified the following:

Major facts: instructor centered teaching; content centered teaching; student centered teaching.

Major issues: Teaching is a highly personal activity. Variety of style is important.

Thesis: Although no one can tell me how to teach, there are a few basic methods I should use on a regular basis to hold the interest of my students.

Prioritize the new information. What seems to be important based on past classes, teacher emphasis, and text readings? Is there a potential exam question here? (See Module 9.)

In the previous example, my students would have noticed that I left the answer to "What is the best teaching style?" up to them. This clearly correlated with my style throughout the semester. Their priorities would be to identify the types of teaching styles, and then to connect them to an overall philosophy of teaching.

Look for groupings and connections. Attempt to establish categories of data. For instance, if you are given a list of 25 items to remember, "chunk" the terms into three or four major categories. In a history class, it might be helpful to group philosophers, scientists, and political leaders. Or how about the following French vocabulary list?

SUCCESS
STRATEGY

aimer mieux (v)	lorsque (adv)
l'anorak (n)	le peuple (n)
le bateau (n)	porter (v)
bientôt (adv)	prochain (adj)
célébrer (v)	puissant (adj)
le danger (n)	le roi (n)
la devise (n)	tricolore (adj)
entouré (adj)	

Rearranged according to parts of speech, the list looks like this:

NOUNS	VERBS	ADJECTIVES	ADVERBS
l'anorak	aimer mieux	entouré	bientôt
le bateau	célébrer	prochain	lorsque
le danger	porter	puissant	
la devise		tricolore	
le peuple			
le roi			

Now, instead of learning 15 isolated items, you have "chunked" the material into a more bite-sized four categories of fewer words, each category with no more than six words.

"I've tried all this stuff, but I still don't understand the new math formula," you say. Well, the good news is you have at least identified what you do *not* know. Try to "talk" a math problem through step-by-step. If possible, do this with someone who is *not* knowledgeable about the topic. This will force you to fully explain each step. Activity 5.6 will help you analyze a problematic topic. Remember, the best way to learn something is to teach it.

ACTIVITY 5.6 — STEP-BY-STEP ANALYSIS OF A PROBLEMATIC TOPIC

Pick a topic (any course) you are currently studying *and* having difficulty understanding. Explain it, step-by-step, in writing below. Then explain it verbally to a classmate. Draw a picture if it helps. The point is to get into the practical details of the topic.

1. Topic with which I am struggling:

_____

_____

_____

2. My step-by-step explanation:

_____

_____

_____

_____

_____

_____

_____

_____

3. What am I still unsure about when it comes to this topic? (Be specific and then ask your instructor for help if you can't find the solution anywhere else.):

_____

_____

_____

_____

_____

_____

_____

Managing your studies with a notebook

SUCCESS STRATEGY

Great notes are useless if you can't find them. Use a notebook for organization. Students have used the following guide successfully. A well-organized notebook is extremely useful when it comes time to studying for finals and national exams (such as those administered by the College Board and the Educational Testing Service), or even in future courses.

Your notebook can, and should be, a vital learning tool for you. The key, however, is found in one word: *organization*. Get rid of those "stuff-it-in-the-pocket" folders. They may have a place every so often, but they tend to be agents of chaos more times than not. They may be efficient but they are not necessarily effective. The following are some pointers students have found helpful:

1. Have a separate three-ring binder (or whatever type of notebook your instructor allows) for each class. Nothing can be more frustrating than trying to find English notes buried in the midst of information on the life of the Roman emperors.

2. Place the course name, classroom number, time of class, and your name on the front cover.

3. In the first section of the notebook, include all general, yet important, handouts. This may include a course description, a listing of term assignments, and a class schedule of homework.

4. Have a separate section for each unit of material. It may be helpful to divide each unit with a tab divider so that it will be easy to find the material. Each unit may contain

   - a summary outline or study guide for the entire unit.
   - daily notes with the date of each class (place this in the upper right-hand corner).
   - handouts that pertain specifically to that unit.
   - quizzes and other graded assignments.
   - the unit exam.

5. File *all* papers in the rings—do not just stick papers in the notebook or textbook. There should always be an established order to follow.

6. Keep a grade sheet. This can take on a very simple three-column format:

   <u>Assignment</u>   <u>Points Earned</u>   <u>Points Possible</u>

   You will always know your grade.

7. Make the notebook work for you. Keep it current and review it every night. An orderly notebook says something about your seriousness and dedication to the course. It also helps you to prepare daily for your next exam. This in turn will reduce test anxiety.

These strategies can also be used for a workplace-related notebook. Have one section containing meeting notes, another holding the notes from phone conferences, and still a third organizing follow-up notes from your in-person calls.

Practice

Practice is extremely important. The strategies we examine here and in other modules will not do anyone any good if they are not used. Moreover, not every strategy is for you. Select according to your learning style and then practice, practice, practice. A basketball coach will show you the best way to toss in a jump shot, a guitar instructor will show you strumming techniques, and your teachers continually give instructions to help in the classroom. However, if you do not practice, you will not progress.

The same is true with study skills. Practice may not make perfect, but as one of my former students once said, practice will make permanent.[6]

A QUICK REVIEW

Before we go any further, take a moment to review what we have covered in the first five modules. Let's apply one of the strategies you have learned in this module—the TSD strategy. For each of the following points, write a one- or two-sentence summary of its contribution to better academic performance:

1. Learning styles:

2. Motivational goals:

3. Time management:

4. Teacher expectations:

5. Clear and organized notes:

---

[6]As with most teachers, I have learned so much from my students. This pearl of wisdom comes by way of a former student and still close friend, Terry Kaden.

Now compare your answers with those below:

1. Learning styles:

   By identifying and applying strategies that are specific to my way of learning, I will get the most out of my study time.

2. Motivational goals:

   By having a clear plan of what I want, when I want it, and how I am going to get it, I will be able to get an A on my English book review.

3. Time management:

   By learning to plan, organize, and make efficient use of time, I will be able to narrow my topic, do initial research followed by a rough outline, do further research, write the first draft, and finally have a friend review it.

4. Teacher expectations:

   By being thoroughly familiar with teacher guidelines and requirements for the project, I will be able to enhance my performance.

5. Clear and organized notes:

   By understanding the big picture and continually reviewing, relating, and reorganizing my notes as I gather more information, I will be better prepared for exams.

Let's also use an analogy of taking a trip to review our topics:

- *Learning styles* help you pick the best method of travel.
- *Motivational goals* help identify the direction in which you wish to travel. You need to know where you are going.
- *Time management* provides the plan of how to get to your desired destination.
- Identifying the *expectations* of the people with whom you are traveling (working) is necessary preparation for the journey so you can get the most out of the experience.
- *Clear and organized notes* of the journey allow you to "revisit" anytime you choose without having to do a lot of work again.

In other words, successful students are able to do the following in and out of the classroom (and in workplace situations as well):

- Identify and work with teacher (manager) expectations.
- Adjust to varying teacher (manager) styles.

- Review class (workplace) activities (lecture notes, video presentation, oral reports) each night.
- Relate and reorganize new information each day.
- Quickly and effectively deal with distractions.
- Actively and appropriately become involved in class (work-related) activities.
- Ask appropriate questions.
- Keep track of all homework assignments.
- Select and consistently use an effective note-taking strategy.
- Keep an organized notebook.

Take a few moments now to review Exhibits 5.6 and 5.7.

exhibit 5.6   Some possible correlations with learning styles.

TOPIC	AUDITORY	KINESTHETIC	VISUAL
Teacher style	A lecture is probably best.	Physical manipulation of class concepts.	Demonstration.
Avoiding distractions	Ask questions and participate.	Hold something in your hand (e.g., a beanbag) but don't let it become a distraction.	Focus on the process of writing notes; draw when appropriate to illustrate notes.
Note taking	A traditional outline may work the best, or some variation.	Use flash cards or index cards that can be manipulated and sorted.	Illustrate your notes by putting a word description on one half of the page and drawings on the other; "organized doodling."
3Rs	Tape the important points and play back; explain your notes to a buddy; discuss the material in a study group.	As you're reviewing, try walking around the room; physically reshuffle the notes; watch a video to reinforce the notes; do an experiment when appropriate; whenever possible, "do" something rather than just "write" something.	Make margin outlines in your notes; draw flow charts and timelines; watch a video.

How to complement selected intelligences.

exhibit 5.7

WHEN GIVEN AN ASSIGNMENT OR TASK, IF YOU ARE STRONG IN . . .	THEN ASK YOURSELF . . .
Intrapersonal intelligence/ choosing instructors	"How can I use this intelligence to pick an instructor's class that complements my learning style?"
Spatial intelligence/ notebook	"How can I use this ability to design a notebook that works for me?"
Linguistic intelligence/ TSDs	"How can I use my language abilities to reorganize my notes effectively?"

Here are some things you can do to improve your learning environment:

- Seek lighting and temperature that are appropriate to your learning style.
- Bring a sweater to class; dress in layers.
- When possible, choose an instructor suited to your style.
- Determine whether you work better on a full stomach or an empty one.
- If possible, schedule classes to coincide with your energy levels.
- Try to schedule study time during an optimum time of day.

Complete the following exercises.

1. Evaluate Disraeli's quote at the beginning of this module.

_____

_____

_____

2. Which of the following characteristics are shared by most successful students when it comes to classroom behavior? (You may circle more than one item.)

   A. They are punctual for class.
   B. When completing another class's homework during the teacher lecture, they do it very quietly so as not to interrupt the instructor.
   C. They miss very few classes.
   D. They realize that it is the teacher's responsibility to tell them about make-up work.
   E. They always put the instructor "on the spot." After all, isn't that what participation is all about?

3. When it comes to notes, the 3Rs refer to
   A. reading, 'riting, 'rithmetic.
   B. review, rewrite, and relate.
   C. review, relate, reorganize.
   D. review, reinvent, reinvigorate.

4. List three strategies to use when you still have problems getting the "big picture":
   A. _____

   B. _____

   C. _____

5. Why is it important to complete the 3Rs on a regular basis?

   _____

   _____

   _____

6. Give three reasons why it is vital to understand an instructor's teaching style and emphasis:
   A. _____

   B. _____

   C. _____

7. How can the TSD method help you in class?

   _____

   _____

   _____

Checklist

Checklist of Selected Tips and Strategies

As a last review, collaborate with a classmate and write a brief description of how each of the following will help you become a more successful student.

THE CLASSROOM EXPERIENCE

1. Practicing

   _____
   _____
   _____

2. Understanding teacher style

   _____
   _____
   _____

3. Understanding teacher expectations

   _____
   _____
   _____

4. Understanding the importance of homework

   _____
   _____
   _____

5. Having your tools

   _____
   _____
   _____

6. Having a positive classroom attitude

   _____
   _____
   _____

7. Coping with distractions: Concentration

   _____
   _____
   _____

8. Coping with distractions: Imagination

_____

_____

_____

9. Coping with distractions: Immediate response

_____

_____

_____

10. Being "cool"

_____

_____

_____

11. Learning actively

_____

_____

_____

12. Using tape recorders, television, and notes

_____

_____

_____

13. Listening actively

_____

_____

_____

14. Note taking: Traditional outline

_____

_____

_____

15. Note taking: Cluster notes/flow-chart notes

_____

_____

_____

16. Note taking: Side-by-side notes

17. Note taking: "Scatter" notes

18. Note taking: Being consistent

19. Using ongoing study guides

20. Implementing the 3Rs

21. Establishing TSDs

22. Having a notebook

READING WITH A PURPOSE

I have to read 1,000 pages by when?

"That must be wonderful; I have no idea what it means."

—MOLIÈRE, 17TH CENTURY FRENCH DRAMATIST

MODULE 6

Overview of This Module

ESTABLISHING THE READING OBJECTIVE

It has happened to all of us. You did your homework but you don't remember what you just read. Or you didn't know what material was most important to remember. So, you tried to remember everything, got overwhelmed, and felt like you wasted your time! That's as frustrating as studying for an exam and still getting a poor grade.

I read my assignment! So, why don't I know what I read?

If you were asked to clean the garage (or the office files, or your room, or the backyard), would you just start working anyplace, moving anything? Probably not. You most likely would want to know exactly what should be moved, thrown away, put away, or cleaned. In other words, you would want to know what the *purpose or end result* of your work should be. The same holds true for reading.

Why do you forget what you read? Recognize the following reasons, and try to do something about them:

- You did not understand the material.
- You did not learn earlier material.
- You did not know what to remember.
- You did not have the right attitude when reading.
- You got bored.
- You read inefficiently.
- You could not establish relationships.
- You did not have an adequate vocabulary to understand the material.

You cannot possibly (nor do you want to) memorize everything you are reading. Remember that the initial reading of an assignment is not the same as studying. When completing your assignment, you are trying to get an understanding of the big picture. Don't get caught in the trap of trying to play Trivial Pursuit with your reading.

It does not make sense to read everything in the same manner, because different books require different strategies. A science book with lots of facts and a strange vocabulary is not read like your history text or your favorite novel. Recognize the differences and make adjustments. The key to increased reading comprehension is to know what the result should be. There are, essentially, six purposes or reasons for reading:[1]

SUCCESS STRATEGY

1. to answer specific questions
2. to apply the reading material (use it in new situations)
3. to find details
4. to get a message
5. to evaluate the reading material (make a judgment)
6. to entertain you

Whatever the purpose, give yourself plenty of *appropriate* breaks so you don't become exhausted.

Identifying the purpose

The all-important question is, How do you know what the purpose of a reading assignment is? Well, if you have been paying any attention in class, this should not be a problem. The teacher most always gives clues. The textbook certainly will also. Remember the 80/20 principle (Module 4)? Well, let's apply it here.

Suppose you have a 50-page reading assignment for your history instructor tonight. That's a lot to read. However, if 80 percent of what you need to know is in approximately 20 percent of the pages, your reading will be reduced to 10 pages. If it takes you three minutes to read a page, you will have just saved yourself two hours of work! Of course, I'm not advocating that you skip pages, only that you can spend more time on the pertinent sections. This is another example of prioritizing. Let me illustrate.

Among the courses I teach is United States History. My emphasis is to show students developing relationships throughout our nation's political, social, and economic development. One area I have never given much class time to is military history. One chapter of a recent textbook consisted of 25 pages covering the years 1861–1865. Fifteen of those pages (60 percent of the total) dealt with Civil War military campaigns. The successful students in my class recognized this fact and did not concentrate on those pages, instead devoting more time to the political and social consequences of those years, the areas they knew I would be testing them on.

SUCCESS STRATEGY

If you can identify the purpose of the assignments from the outset, there is less of a chance of being overwhelmed by extraneous data. As you advance through school, more will be expected and assigned. Learn now how to take well-calculated shortcuts, but don't equate this with the "easy way out." Shortcuts are simply a more efficient manner to attain your goals.

---

[1]Ron Fry, *Improve Your Reading,* 18.

Here's another example. If I asked you to find the phone number for Dominic Jones at 123 Maple Leaf Lane, what would you do? Would you pick up the phone book and start reading from the *A*s? I doubt it. Why not? Because it would be a waste of your time. You would search for the *J*s, then scan for his last name, and finally for his full name until you found it. Why read what is not necessary? The same principle should hold true for your school assignments. Likewise, this is a skill that can be used beyond school—on your job, in your pleasure reading, or in deciding on a vacation spot.

Tackling a reading assignment

Before beginning practice or entering an actual game situation, athletes warm up by performing calisthenics and stretching exercises to limber up their muscles. Reading should be no different. If you just open your book to the assigned page and start reading, you have started running without warming up. Don't be a passive reader, mindlessly going through the motions as you drift from page to page like a leaf blown by the wind. Move with a purpose!

DEALING WITH A BORING TEXTBOOK

Unfortunately, most textbooks are dry and sleep inducing. One would think authors get a bonus for writing boring and encyclopedic volumes. Like it or not, your teachers *will* expect you to read the assignments. What is a student to do?

How does the instructor expect me to get through this boring textbook?

If you are like most students, you probably have asked this question many times during your school years. It will not be easy, but if you follow the plan in Activity 6.1, you will not only "get through" the dullest of textbooks, but you will also retain more than you ever thought possible. Moreover, if this works for boring books, think of the results with exciting works you want to read.

There is nothing magical about this approach. I have used it with my students for years. Others[2] have written about it. It is a commonsense approach successful students have used for years. But you must have desire to accomplish it.

The Plan

More than five decades ago, F. P. Robinson developed a reading strategy that has been duplicated ever since.[3] The technique, known as SQ3R (survey, question, read, review, recite), is the basis for the following plan. Most study skills books have some variation of this plan. Call it what you will, there are essentially three stages to the plan: preread, read, and postread.

---

[2]For instance, Adam Robinson, *What Smart Students Know* (New York: Crown Trade Paperbacks, 1993), 36–37.

[3]Franklin Pleasant Robinson developed the now famous SQ3R method during World War II. The first edition of his book *Effective Study* was published in 1946. A fourth edition was published by Harper & Row in 1970.

A PLAN FOR SUCCESSFULLY COMPLETING A READING ASSIGNMENT ACTIVITY 6.1

Date: _____

Class: _____ Assigned pages: _____

Select one of your textbooks in which you currently have a reading assignment. Below write the steps you normally would take to complete the assignment. When you finish, compare your answers with a classmate. Then read the plan in the next section.

My steps to successfully completing a reading activity:

Step 1: _____

_____

_____

Step 2: _____

_____

_____

Step 3: _____

_____

_____

Step 4: _____

_____

_____

Step 5: _____

_____

_____

Step 6: _____

_____

_____

Step 7: _____

_____

_____

Step 8: _____

_____

_____

SUCCESS STRATEGY

PREREAD

1. **Establish a purpose.** Do you have a target? Or are you just wandering through the passage to be read? If you sit down to read your assignment but have no earthly idea why you are reading or what you are looking for, you might as well turn on the TV and watch a football game. If you don't know what to look for, the reading can seem like torture.

Ask some basic questions to establish a purpose before starting. For instance, "What is this instructor concentrating on in class?" or "What kind of test questions might evolve from this reading?" Telling yourself "I gotta read cause my teacher told me to" is *not* a purpose.

2. **Warm up your intellectual muscles.** Now, stretch those mind muscles. You need to actively prepare to read. To accomplish this do the following:

- Sit on the edge of your seat, literally. This sends a signal that you are ready to engage actively in work.
- Quickly review in your mind (or by opening your class notes) what you have covered in class to date on the topic before you in the text.
- Relate as best you can how this material might connect to the overall emphasis in the classroom. In other words, use past knowledge to ground you in the reading *and* to establish memory hooks for this new material (more on this in Module 8.)

3. **Skim and scan.** Still warming up, quickly flip through the pages of the assignment. Skimming provides a quick feel for what the big picture is. What you want is a general sense of the assignment. Read the introduction and the summary of the chapter. If you have to accomplish a certain outcome by the end of your reading—say, answer teacher-provided questions—then scan the material with this particular purpose in mind.

This strategy, though it adds a little time to the front end of your reading, will aid comprehension and trim time from the overall reading assignment. Once you finish this prereading activity, you will have a better idea what you need to read—and what you can skip! Remember the 80/20 principle (Module 4).

Skimming includes the following steps:

- Read the chapter's introductory section and summary. Unlike a good mystery novel, you want to know where this reading is going to lead you.
- Read the chapter's headings/subheadings and form questions based on them. These questions will give you a *purpose* for reading. You will be actively looking for information.
- Look at all pictures, graphics, and captions. The author put them in the text for a reason.
- Look at boldfaced, italicized, and underlined terms. They are high-lighted for a purpose.
- Look at the end-of-chapter terms and questions (if available).

The following headings are the actual chapter and unit headings from a review book on United States history.[4] As you read these chapter guideposts,

---
[4]Piscitelli, 2001, 127–39.

ask yourself, "How would I use this information? What type of questions can I develop from this information?"

An Era of Sacrifice and Adjustment, 1929–1952

The Great Depression

FDR & the New Deal

Interwar Maneuverings: Attempts to Avoid Another War

Diplomacy Fails: World War II

The United States Assumes a New International Role: The Cold War and Its Consequences

Let's tackle this task with purpose and effectiveness. Here are some possible questions using the headings:

An Era of Sacrifice and Adjustment, 1929–1952

Who was sacrificing? What was being adjusted? How were the sacrifices made? Why was there sacrifice during this time? What is an era?

The Great Depression

What was the Great Depression? What caused the Great Depression? How did people cope with this? What is a "depression"? Who was affected most by the Great Depression? Why did the Great Depression occur during this time?

FDR & the New Deal

Who is FDR? What did he do? What was his connection to the Great Depression? What was the New Deal? When was the New Deal introduced? Why was the New Deal introduced? Who was involved with the New Deal?

Interwar Maneuverings: Attempts to Avoid Another War

Who was maneuvering? Why were they maneuvering? How did this connect with the above topics? What were the consequences of these maneuvers? Was there another war? If so, what war was it?

Diplomacy Fails: World War II

Why did diplomacy fail? Who was involved with the diplomacy? Was this connected to the Great Depression? How did this affect FDR?

The United States Assumes a New International Role: The Cold War and Its Consequences

What was the new role for the United States? How was this different from past roles? Why did the United States assume this new role? What was the Cold War? Who was involved in this war? How was the Cold War different from other wars? Why was this war "cold"?

"But I thought these strategies would shorten reading time!" you cry out. Any new skill is awkward at first. It takes practice for it to become habit. Your reading comprehension should increase with more effective reading strategies. Take a few minutes now to complete Activity 6.2.

ACTIVITY 6.2   DEVELOPING YOUR OWN QUESTIONS FROM CHAPTER HEADINGS

Develop your own questions for the following headings taken from the same book on United States history.[5] The main idea is to establish direction for your reading.

From Affluence to Turbulence and Reaction, 1952–1980

_____

_____

_____

The Eisenhower Years: The Mystique of Affluence

_____

_____

_____

Camelot and the Great Society: Turbulence

_____

_____

_____

Nixon: The Silent Majority Acts

_____

_____

_____

From Nixon to Reagan: Still More Reaction

_____

_____

_____

_____

[5]Piscitelli, 140–156.

4. **Give yourself some tasks.** You need to spice up the chore of book reading. Send yourself on a fact-finding mission. What is the important stuff? Use all clues that have been provided. If you are given a study guide, use it! If not, make your own. You have already turned all those chapter headings and subheadings into questions. This gives you a purpose, as you now must answer those questions. Review captions and graphics. Look at the end-of-the-chapter terms. In short, ask yourself, "What do I need to know?"

Be an investigative reporter and ask *who? what? when? why? where? how?* Refer (again) to the 80/20 principle. Obviously, class attendance will help here. See, how everything is beginning to fall into place now?

READ

SUCCESS STRATEGY

5. **Read (finally!).** It's one thing to do all of the preparation work called for in steps 1 through 4, but it's quite another to take notes of the reading. "Just write good notes on the main points" does not help if you cannot figure out what the main points are in the reading selection. A few suggestions are particularly pertinent at this juncture of your reading assignment:

- Refer to the questions you posed in step 3. For instance, "What caused the Great Depression?" As you read, note the main factors that brought about the Great Depression. Can you further divide each of the causes? If so, make a note. Think of this process as the reverse of the writing process. Instead of building a body around a skeleton (the outline), you are picking the meat (main points) from the bones.

- If you generally have difficulty understanding the central idea of an assignment, read one section at a time. Stop after each section and write a brief summary. Start with one paragraph, and move on to longer sections as you become more skilled.

- Clump two or more headings together in order to develop relationships. Your comparison could take the form of either flow-chart notes or a data retrieval chart (see Module 8).

- Pay particular attention to the words that give you trouble. These words may be the very ones the author is using for a significant reason. This sound advice comes from Mortimer J. Adler and Charles Van Doren, in their classic work *How to Read a Book*. They state, "From your point of view as a reader, therefore, the most important words are *those that give you trouble*" (author's emphasis).[6]

  In other words, if a word appears awkward, unusual, or strange within the context, there is a good likelihood that it's an important term. This is not foolproof, but if you pay attention to the context of the paragraph, you will have a better chance of determining the main point.

- Keep a dictionary handy. This will slow the reading pace at first, but if you don't know the words, it's difficult to understand the meaning.

- Don't forget your English training. Look for the topic sentence of each paragraph. Let this guide your reading notes. Remember, you can find a topic sentence in the beginning, middle, or end of a paragraph. (Some authors may *not* even *write* one; it is implied.)

---

[6]Mortimer Adler and Charles Van Doren, *How to Read a Book* (New York: Simon & Schuster, 1972), 102.

- Don't read the texts of different disciplines in the same manner.[7] Once you realize that not all texts are created equally, it will be easier to find the main point.

  - When reading a *history* text, look for cause and effect, important people, impact of events on people, turning points, and hints of bias or prejudice by the author.
  - A *science* book may be more apt to focus on classifications, experimental steps, hypotheses, and unexplained phenomena.
  - That *English* novel you have been struggling with is bound to have symbolism, character thresholds, a hero, tragic flaws, and a developing message.
  - And, yes, even *math* books have their particular characteristics. You may need to know which variables, functions, theorems, and axioms are the building blocks of the chapter.

A word about highlighting: If you choose to highlight or underline text, be careful. You want to highlight the major points. Too many students just paint the page yellow. This is useless. Note taking is more effective because it forces you to encode the material, to put the material into your own words. If you can do this, you *understand* it.

SUCCESS STRATEGY

POSTREAD

6. **Don't shut that book yet.** When you have completed the reading, *immediately* take 5 or 10 minutes to study the notes you just wrote. It has been stated that 80 percent of what you just read can be lost within 24 hours if you don't review (see Module 8). Organize and reorganize your notes according to categories, theories, trends, or some other grouping. What is the big picture? Can you hook this new knowledge to previously learned material? Can you see any relationships emerging? This step will be a blessing in the long run. It keeps you on task, while also preparing you for the next class as well as the coming exam. If you are confused about the reading, bring your question(s) to the next class. Maybe, just maybe, you won't have to do any last-minute cramming.

7. **Bring your reading outline to class.** You are now ready to answer questions, follow the instructor's presentation, and ask your own questions. And since you will be looking at the material for (at least) the second time, you will also be studying on the instructor's time. Now, that's efficient!

Have you ever had an instructor who is always on a tangent; that is, he or she is constantly getting off the subject? Or one who never seems to have a focus? By coming to class prepared, you will be in a better position to follow and understand a rambling presentation. In this manner, you are taking responsibility for your learning.

I have seen students come to class, open their textbook—for the first time—and attempt to follow the lesson *and* search for answers to teacher questions. If you do this, you might as well raise your hand and tell the instructor, "Mr. Peabody, I didn't do the assignment but your presentation is so dull and predictable I can do it now."

8. **Utilize supplemental sources.** If you are still having a difficult time with the textbook, try looking for other sources. For instance, most bookstores sell short

---

[7]Ibid. Chapters 13 and 19, passim.

versions of American history. Such books concentrate on the major points of historical periods. The same holds true for books in other disciplines. *CliffsNotes* present the major points for novels and plays. What you are getting with these supplemental books is an outline of major points. This *should not be a substitute,* but it can help you get through all of the superfluous material.

The point here is *not* to try to beat the system. It's to help you organize and succeed. (In any case, teachers know what is in the *CliffsNotes,* and their test questions will definitely go beyond this source. Trying to find the *easy* way may not be the *best* way.)

Well, there you have it. Nothing is "guaranteed" but this is an achievable plan. The benefits are many. The notes you develop while reading, for instance, will serve as an excellent guide for your classroom notes. With your reading complete and organized, you are then armed and ready for the teacher's presentation. You can participate; you can be actively learning. It takes effort—but you did say you wanted better grades. And you will be able to use your precious time more effectively.

Finally, note that steps 1 through 4 are warm-ups. These steps represent a preread activity. Step 5 requires the reader to focus and concentrate on the material at hand. The 80/20 principle comes in here. And the last three steps are important because they will help you develop relationships that, as we said earlier, are important for comprehension.

Now, what do I do with my reading notes?

Now that you have mastered this reading assignment, what can you do with the notes you have? Bring them to class. Using reading notes in class serves a variety of purposes. These notes can

- serve as a guide for discussion.
- help you answer teacher-posed questions.
- remind you to ask clarifying questions.
- allow you to focus on the important points the teacher is making.

If you are familiar with the material, taking notes will be that much easier to accomplish. You will be more prepared to listen and participate actively.

If you will recall, doing homework is not necessarily studying. Completing the homework is the first step. But you need to review, reorganize, and find relationships as you study. If you take the reading notes to class, they automatically become a study aid. As you review the notes in class, you are, in effect, studying on the teacher's time. No more cramming for an exam!

One last strategy on this topic. As a reflective self-assessment, ask yourself if you could intelligently discuss the reading material in class discussion. If you can, congratulate yourself. If you can't, you may wish to review the assignment briefly before you get to class. Remember that practice makes permanent.

**SUCCESS
STRATEGY**

My instructor always falls behind schedule

Instructors have great intentions. They meticulously plan a unit of study, neatly matching and spacing reading assignments to complement well-thought-out lectures and activities. The climax is the unit exam.

Unfortunately, great plans get lost in the realities of day-to-day classroom business. Have you ever had an instructor who painstakingly covered one chapter in three *weeks,* only to finish the unit with a "big push" to cover four chapters in three *days?* This introduces an element of stress for everyone concerned, but *you* have to deal with it.

While it's best to do homework reading that corresponds with classroom topics (for example, preparing for the lesson prior to coming to class), don't wait to digest 90 pages of new material in a couple of nights. Put yourself on a schedule (see Module 4), read, and keep the outlines handy for when the teacher finally reviews material in class.

I've followed the plan but my reading comprehension is still lousy!

You might find the following prescription far from a miracle cure. In fact, you might find it downright uncomfortable, but give it a chance.

- *Build your vocabulary (part I).* This means using a dictionary to clarify meanings. Look up new words, correct misspellings on exams and homework, and become familiar with synonyms and antonyms. A pocket-sized dictionary and thesaurus are two of the most valuable yet inexpensive books you should have on your desk.

- *Build your vocabulary (part II).* Take about 15 minutes in the morning to work on the daily crossword puzzle in the newspaper. This has two benefits: (1) it helps to build your vocabulary, and (2) it limbers up your "mental muscles" for the coming academic day.

The reading plan is fine for textbooks, but what about novels?

That is a good question. Most novels do not provide the reader with neat headings and subheadings. Chapters might only be identified by a number rather than a descriptive title. Planning the reading attack will be more difficult, but not impossible. It just takes some creativity. I have seen the following techniques work.

- Once you have completed reading a chapter, give it your own title. Whatever title you choose, it should answer the question, "What is the main point of this chapter?" Be as creative and descriptive as you can.

- Why was the chapter written? Briefly summarize the purpose of the chapter and its connection to the rest of the book. Closely tied to this is a brief summary of what happened and why? Even if you can't identify the plot, this will help point you in the general direction.

- Identify any characters introduced, their relationship with other characters, their significance, and their connection to the plot. Did anyone utter a particularly meaningful statement? (You know how English instructors love to ask *who* said *what* to whom *when, where,* and *why.*) Some students have found charactergrams beneficial. Think of a charactergram as a word diagram of the characters' traits and importance to the story. For those who

An example of a charactergram.   *exhibit 6.1*

CHAPTER 1
"My creative title"

Character 1	*Character 2*	*Character 3*
When:	When:	When:
Connection to another:	Connection to another:	Connection to another:
Significant quote:	Significant quote:	Significant quote:
Symbolism:	Symbolism:	Symbolism:

Brief chapter summary:

_____

_____

_____

Confusing points:

_____

_____

_____

---

learn better with pictures and diagrams, the example in Exhibit 6.1 may be particularly useful.

- Be sensitive to symbols. Is water being used to depict rebirth, or an old animal synonymous with dying, or autumn representative of old age? Add these to the charactergram as appropriate.

- Finally, make a note of what you do *not* understand. Be as specific as possible. Ask a friend or the instructor for guidance.

A QUICK REVIEW

This module presented efficient reading strategies to improve comprehension. Always know your purpose for reading. Be sure to warm up first by doing a quick skim of the material in front of you. Find the big picture—the main idea. Finally, evaluate *your* reading comprehension. Are you ready to participate in class?

If you follow the tips in this module, you will be much closer to becoming an active learner, rather than a passive receptacle waiting for the teacher to act on you.

Going back to our analogy of taking a trip in Module 5, you can easily see how all of this ties together. Remember, we are trying to be as efficient as possible.

- You need to know where you are going before you leave.
- You need to map out the most effective way to get there.
- Your notes of the trip will allow easy and quick review of the trip so you don't have to travel over the same long territory again.
- You need to read actively (your map, road signs). Know your purpose and go after it. If you don't know what to look for, you certainly will get lost!

Specifically, the successful student is able to

- identify a purpose for reading an assignment.
- effectively skim and scan a reading assignment.
- succinctly summarize a reading passage in his or her own words.
- use supplemental sources to complement a reading assignment.
- continually build his or her vocabulary.

Take a few minutes now to review Exhibits 6.2 and 6.3.

exhibit 6.2   **Some possible correlations with your learning style.**

TOPIC	AUDITORY	KINESTHETIC	VISUAL
Prereading	Write or tape-record questions to guide your reading.	Put questions on flash cards and physically manipulate as you find answers to your questions.	Write questions; highlight key words.
Reading	Outline notes.	Underline and/or highlight; draw charts or time lines.	Outline notes; draw charts or time lines.
Supplemental sources	Listen to prerecorded tapes of texts.	Watch videos.	Look at pictures or videos.
Reading novels	Create an outline; use margin notes.	Write important information on index cards.	Create flow charts and charactergrams.

How to complement selected intelligences.

exhibit 6.3

WHEN GIVEN AN ASSIGNMENT OR TASK, IF YOU ARE STRONG IN . . .	THEN ASK YOURSELF . . .
Interpersonal intelligence/ postreading	"How can I use my abilities to work with other people to help me review my reading for comprehension?"
Bodily-kinesthetic intelligence/ reading with a purpose	"How can I use my ability with role plays and movement to help me read with greater comprehension?"
Naturalistic intelligence/ reading with a purpose	"How can I use my abilities to categorize my environment to help me understand my reading assignment?"

Here are some things you can do to improve your learning environment:

- Be sure your study space has the appropriate lighting and comfort level.
- Try to read at a time of day when your energy level is at its highest.

Complete the following exercises.

1. Evaluate Molière's quote at the beginning of the module.

   _____

   _____

   _____

2. Which of the following is *not* a reason why you might forget what you read?
   A. You did not understand the material.
   B. You did not want to understand the material.
   C. You could easily establish relationships.
   D. Your vocabulary was limited.

3. List three of the six purposes of reading:
   A. _____
   B. _____
   C. _____

4. What does SQ3R stand for?

S: _____

Q: _____

R: _____

R: _____

R: _____

5. What strategy provides a general sense of the reading assignment—in other words, a quick feel for what the big picture is?

_____

_____

_____

6. Explain the charactergram strategy. How can it help you wade through a novel and help you comprehend the plot?

_____

_____

_____

Checklist

Checklist of Selected Tips and Strategies

As a last review, collaborate with a classmate and write a brief description of how each of the following will help you become a more successful student.

READING STRATEGIES

1. Establishing a purpose

_____
_____
_____

2. Understanding different books = different approaches

_____
_____
_____

3. Focusing on ideas

_____
_____
_____

4. Warming up

_____
_____
_____

5. Skimming

_____
_____
_____

6. Scanning

_____
_____
_____

7. Establishing questions

_____
_____
_____

8. Establishing tasks

9. Taking notes on reading

10. Bringing your outline to class

11. Using supplemental sources

12. Building your vocabulary

13. Using charactergrams

"True eloquence consists in saying all that is proper and nothing more."

—FRANCOIS DE LA ROCHEFOUCAULD, SEVENTEENTH-CENTURY FRENCH AUTHOR

MODULE 7

Overview of This Module

STATING IT, SUPPORTING IT, CONCLUDING IT, AND EVALUATING IT

Your English instructor knows best

Recently, I walked into a colleague's campus office. This English instructor's wall was lined from corner to corner with every conceivable text on writing style, techniques, strategies, and the like. There seemed to be a gazillion books. The point? For the most part, you will receive competent writing instruction from your English department. The purpose of this module is not to teach you how to write. Such an endeavor is beyond the scope of this book. The intent is to introduce and reinforce some basic strategies. These techniques will help with homework writing assignments and essay exams (see Module 9).

If you will remember, Module 6 stressed that you must know your purpose before you start to read. Knowing the purpose helps to guide your approach so that you may effectively and efficiently accomplish the assigned task. The same holds true for writing.

Before writing, you need to know why you are writing. What does your teacher expect from your efforts? There are various types and styles of writing.

You will, at one point or another in your classroom career, be asked to write essays that are descriptive, narrative, comparative, or argumentative. Some essays focus on how to do something, while others are concentrated on describing cause and effect.

Keep in mind that this section does not cover each style of writing. We will look at basic writing strategies designed to get you *started*. In particular, we will review the basic five-paragraph argumentative or persuasive essay. This essay style attempts to prove a point. Many exam essays are of this nature.

But a word of caution. There is a point at which the five-paragraph format is inappropriate, rigid, and restrictive. Don't get caught in the mind-set that you can only write five paragraphs. Some prompts might actually ask you to address four or five points. (The prompt is what some call the "essay question.") Your essay can easily be longer than five paragraphs.

Don't be a slave to a formula. There are, however, some basic rules to get you started.

I always think my essay is great—too bad my instructor doesn't share the same view

SUCCESS STRATEGY

Before you start writing, plan your response. As with any topic, always make sure you know what your instructor wants before you start writing. Read the instructions *aloud* (when appropriate). Make sure you *hear* what you are to do. A quick and effective method is to "mark up" the prompt. Develop a series of symbols (such as underline, circle, and box) to highlight the key tasks in the essay instructions. Let's analyze the following prompt. The tasks (what you are to do) are underlined, the key issues circled, and other important guidelines are boxed.

"Explain the purpose of the New Colonial System and evaluate its impact on colonial solidarity during the period of 1763–1775."

Once you have accomplished this, a quick outline for the essay response can be developed:

New Colonial System (1763–1775)

- What was it? Describe it.
- Who did it?
- Why was it done?
- Results on solidarity?
  - Describe it.
  - My judgment—good, bad? What criteria will I use?

Now complete Activity 7.1 to get a feel for this process.

ACTIVITY 7.1   ANALYZING A PROMPT AND DEVELOPING AN OUTLINE

Choose an essay prompt from a previous class exam, a current assignment, or one you have developed from your notes. Underline, circle, and box the key information as appropriate. Then develop a rough outline.

_____

_____

_____

_____

_____

_____

_____

_____

_____

_____

_____

SUCCESS STRATEGY

Writing decisions

There is a simple formula for writing, but you have to address certain questions before you start. Do not go into the assignment blindly.

Some of the more basic decisions a writer must make include determinations about

- topic (for our purposes, let's assume the teacher has assigned a topic—the usual situation on an exam).
- an opinion on the topic.
- supporting evidence for the opinion.
- the audience for whom the writing is intended (for our purposes, the teacher).
- the organization of the paper.
- who will proofread the essay (besides you).

Most teacher-assigned essays require a string of related paragraphs that explain, analyze, argue, or persuade the reader about a particular topic. Here is an exercise to get your writing juices flowing.

Look at your T.O.E.S.: The basic components of an essay

T.O.E.S. is an acronym (see Module 8) that will help you remember the main components of a basic essay. Your essay must have a Topic, an Opinion, supporting Evidence, and a Summary. If you ever forget, just look at your TOES! Try the reinforcement exercise in Activity 7.2.

REINFORCING THE CONCEPT OF T.O.E.S.

1. Complete the following:

   (**Topic**) Give the name of one of your best friends—just the name.

   _____

   (**Opinion**) State an opinion about that person.

   _____

   (**Evidence**) List three facts that support your opinion about this individual.

   _____

   _____

   _____

   (**Summary**) Write a one-sentence summary.

   _____

   _____

2. Do the same exercise again, but this time convince someone of something you should be allowed to do.

   T: (What do you want to do?) _____

   O: (Why should you be allowed to do it?) _____

   E: 1. _____

       2. _____

       3. _____

   S: _____

3. Organize an answer to a textbook or lecture question.

   T: _____

   O: _____

   E: 1. _____

       2. _____

       3. _____

   S: _____

Stating it: Thesis statements

What you have just written is the beginning of a thesis or main-idea statement. For some reason, this relatively simple process is an obstacle for lots of young scholars—from middle school through college. There is nothing mystical about it. Read the clarifying remarks in Activity 7.3 and then complete the exercises.

ACTIVITY 7.3 — WRITING MAIN-IDEA (THESIS) STATEMENTS

Every main-idea statement must contain the following:

- The topic.
- Your opinion.
- The direction of your argument (the areas you will use to prove your thesis). Think of this as a "road map" for your reader.

Here are some hints for writing clear thesis statements:

- Be sure to address the topic. This sounds simple but so many students miss this basic point.
- State only one opinion. Do not try to prove two or more arguments. In other words, *focus on your task.*
- Be sure to state an opinion, not just a fact. You will have more success building an argument around an opinion rather than a fact. For example:

  Difficult to argue: The Yankees are a baseball team. (fact)

  Easier to argue: The Yankees are the greatest team ever. (opinion)

- Make sure you have provided a brief road map so the reader knows how you plan to develop your opinion. For example:

  Lack of clear direction: The Yankees are the greatest team ever.

  Direction provided: To prove that the Yankees are the greatest team ever, just count the number of star players, games won, and championships claimed.

Exercise 1: Put a check next to the clearly stated thesis statements. Remember to use the criteria established above.

- ⊙ Swimming is a sport.
- ⊙ Students who continually practice note-taking strategies, time-management strategies, and active reading techniques will become more confident students.
- ⊙ This is an effective study skills book.
- ⊙ The successful student.
- ⊙ I am a successful student because I do all of my homework, listen carefully to instructions, and establish realistic goals.

Exercise 2: Rewrite the poorly written thesis statements in Exercise 1.

_____

_____

_____

_____

_____

Exercise 3: For each of the following topics, write an opinion. Remember, you must establish an arguable position. Simply stating "I like my brother" is difficult to argue; it is more a statement of fact.

Study skills

_____

_____

_____

Football

_____

_____

_____

School

_____

_____

_____

Exercise 4: Now that you have established clear opinions, how will you prove them? That is, what points will you use? Revise your sentences below.

_____

_____

_____

_____

_____

_____

Although answers may vary, here are some possible answers for the exercises you just completed.

Exercise 1:

- ○ Swimming is a sport.
- ✓ Students who continually practice note-taking strategies, time-management strategies, and active reading techniques will become more confident students.
- ○ This is an effective study skills book.
- ○ The successful student.
- ✓ I am a successful student because I do all of my homework, listen carefully to instructions, and establish realistic goals.

(continued)

Exercise 2:

- Swimming is a sport that requires great endurance. Every muscle is used because the swimmer must constantly propel himself.
- This is an effective study skills book because it is easy to read, well organized, and provides practical strategies.
- If a student develops efficient time-management skills, purposeful reading techniques, and realistic goals, she will become a successful student.

Exercise 3:

Study skills
Effective study skills separate the successful from the unsuccessful students.

Football
Football is a sport that requires both brain and muscle power.

School
School is a necessary training ground for a productive life.

Exercise 4:

- Effective study skills separate the successful from the unsuccessful student by developing responsible habits, attitudes, and academic strategies.
- The complexity of plays, the coordination of movement among 11 players, along with the brute strength involved proves that football is a sport that requires both brain and muscle power.
- School is a necessary training ground for a productive life because it helps students develop interpersonal relations, communication skills, and vocational abilities.

The items in Activity 7.3 are *rough* examples to illustrate the components of a thesis statement. As you become more sophisticated in your writing, it will become obvious that a thesis statement need not—and probably should not—be limited to one sentence; it will usually encompass a paragraph. Until you get to that point, your teachers will be thrilled with a complete and logical main-idea statement.

Once you can write a basic thesis statement, work on more extensive statements. Your formula might look like this:

- *Step 1: First sentence*—Briefly establish the background, or context, for the topic you are addressing.
- *Step 2: Second, third, and fourth sentences*—Give a broad overview of the points you will use to prove your opinion.
- *Step 3: Fifth sentence*—State your opinion. This is the position you will be proving in the body of the essay.

Note that you can switch the order of steps 2 and 3, but always check with your teacher.

Another way to accomplish this process is by asking yourself questions. For example:

Topic: My best friend Igor.

(Question: Why is Igor my best friend?)

Opinion: Igor is my best friend because he is one of the most compassionate people I have ever met.

(Question: How do I know Igor is so compassionate?)

Evidence: 1. He is always willing to listen.

2. He is ready to help at a moment's notice.

3. He never says a mean word.

Summary: Igor's compassion is evident in thought, word, and deed.

Here is another example taken from the outline given earlier in the module:

T: The New Colonial System.

O: The strict enforcement of Britain's New Colonial System brought the colonists closer than ever before as they united against a common enemy.

E: 1. New imperial legislation was enacted (Sugar and Stamp Acts).

2. Colonial meetings were held to map out strategy (Stamp Act Congress).

3. Colonial networking was established (Committees of Correspondence).

S: When England switched from a permissive imperial system to a more stringently enforced program of laws, the colonists became more defiant than ever.

Supporting it: The body of the essay—The 5 x 5 principle

A simple rule of thumb is to develop a five-paragraph essay, with each paragraph consisting of at least five sentences. You have already developed the basis for a thesis paragraph. Now, you have to support that thesis. Everything

SUCCESS STRATEGY

that follows in paragraphs two, three, and four must be directly related to the thesis. If it isn't, you are wasting your time and the teacher's—and you won't get the best grade possible.

Most class essays test your knowledge of material. These essays are *not* the origins of the next great American novel. Keep to the point. All sentences in a paragraph should relate to the topic of the paragraph, and all paragraphs should relate to and support the thesis. To do anything else borders on "fluff"—that is, beyond-the-scope writing.

Once you have a thesis written, it is time to support your position. I'll make one major assumption here: you have knowledge of the material. (Really, there is no substitute for *knowing* the material. Sorry, but you can't expect to illuminate others about a topic if you don't understand it yourself.) The challenge most students face is to organize the data they do have. Why not try clustering?[1]

SUCCESS STRATEGY

This technique is great for making sense out of the information at your fingertips. On a separate piece of paper, write your main topic in the middle of the page. Now, without stopping to organize anything, write all of the subtopics (supporting data) around this topic.

Suppose you had to write an essay about the challenges faced by the new U.S. government following the Revolutionary War. Exhibit 7.1 shows one way you might organize your thoughts.

---

exhibit 7.1   Clustering method showing subtopics.

[SUPPORTING EVIDENCE]
↓
1. Who would rule the government?

[SUPPORTING EVIDENCE]
↓
2. What would replace English industrial goods?

[MAIN TOPIC]
↓
The new national government had to address many critical issues in 1783.

[SUPPORTING EVIDENCE]
↓
3. What type of culture would the new nation have?

---

[1]So many writers and teachers have used this method that I cannot attribute it to one particular individual. For a particularly detailed explanation, I refer the reader to Sheila Bender, *Writing Personal Essays: How to Shape Your Life Experiences for the Page* (Cincinnati, OH: Writer's Digest Books, 1995), passim.

Clustering method showing supporting facts.   *exhibit 7.2*

1. Who would rule the
   government?

   [FACTS]
   ↓

—Weakness in articles of Confederation
—Taxing power
—Raising an army
—Method of picking leaders

2. What would replace English
   industrial goods?

   [FACTS]
   ↓

—No more mercantilism
—Need for $
—International markets

The new national government had to address many critical issues in 1783.

3. What type of culture would
   the new nation have?

   [FACTS]
   ↓
—Gender relationships
—American-style painting
—The American language

Once you have established these major subtopics, it's time to plug in the facts to support your opinion. From the subtopics, draw lines to supporting facts. You can do this in a matter of minutes. Now, take a moment and evaluate what you have. See Exhibit 7.2 for an example.

Once you have completed this part of the clustering diagram, you can use it as a rough outline for your supporting paragraphs. From here, develop each subtopic into a paragraph. Make sure each paragraph supports the thesis in your introductory paragraph.

What do I do about writer's block?

The best-prepared student will "come up empty" at times. You have all your tools but you just can't get moving. Even a well-tuned car with all the options won't leave the driveway unless the battery is cranking.

When your "writing battery" is drained, you need to jump-start it. But how? Ask yourself the following questions to get moving again:

- Can I relate this (the topic, the evidence) to anything else?

**SUCCESS
STRATEGY**

- Are there any groupings or connections?
- What are the consequences of this issue?
- Is this good/positive or bad/negative?
- Do others really care about it? Who?
- How do I feel about it?
- Is this an absolute, or are there counterexamples?
- How does this fit into a bigger picture?

Concluding it: The clincher

Once you have sufficiently established and supported your thesis, it's time for the clincher—time to close the essay with a powerful thought.

Do not just *end* your writing. State the importance of your opinion. Make sure your main point is not missed. A sophisticated conclusion does not just restate the thesis. It may be an effective idea to reemphasize one or two of your key thesis words, but go further than a simple summary. To arrive at a dynamic conclusion, try asking yourself the following questions:

- Why is this topic or opinion important?
- How does my opinion fit into a bigger picture?
- Why is this topic significant?

The big picture

In the beginning of this module, I stated that the formula for an effective essay is relatively simple. For the visual learners in the crowd, Exhibit 7.3 illustrates the flow of the essay. Now let's walk through the process of writing an essay step-by-step.

SUCCESS STRATEGY

GENERAL INFORMATION FOR STANDARD ESSAYS

1. *Read* the prompt. This sounds simple, but don't overlook it. Carefully digest each word of the prompt. What is the topic? What is the setting? Can you identify the *who, what, when, where,* and *why* of the item? Before you start writing, you should very carefully read the essay assignment. What is the prompt asking you to accomplish? Underline your tasks so you don't miss them.

   Following is a partial list of key words—words you are most likely to find in essay prompts. *You need to know these words:*

   analyze: to divide a topic or issue into its parts; to show the relation of one part to another

   apply: use your knowledge in a new or different situation

   assess: to judge the merits of some issue; to evaluate

   classify: to put things into categories

   compare: to provide similarities, differences, consequences (see *analyze*)

   contrast: to provide differences

   criticize: to judge critically

The flow of the essay.

exhibit 7.3

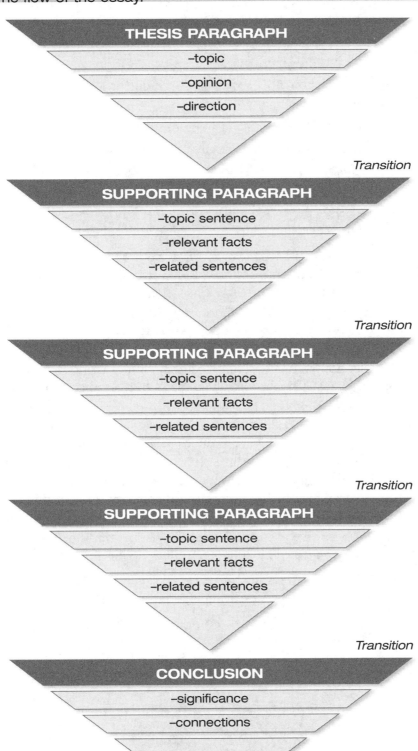

defend: to argue for a particular issue

describe: to explain an event, issue, topic; to explain the main characteristics

discuss: to explain in detail; to go beyond mere description

evaluate: to judge, criticize, establish standards

identify: to show how something is unique or individual

illustrate: to provide examples

interpret: to describe the meaning of an issue

motivations: what caused something to happen

relative importance: how two or more factors compare with one another

summarize: to restate briefly

trace: to provide an order or sequence of events

Make sure you understand these words. Do what the item calls for. If you are asked to describe the consequences of World War II, do not *assess the motivations* for going to war.

2. Say it. Support it. Conclude it. In other words, make sure you have a clear thesis. Provide arguments, or evidence, to support your thesis. Tie the essay together at the end.

3. Logically develop your thesis. Stay focused. Do not use a shotgun approach. Make sure your opinion connects to the topic of the essay.

4. *Before* you write the essay, take a moment to plan your response. Jot down a brief outline. Don't go into a wild writing frenzy. Take a deep breath, think, and *then* write. Use the clustering technique here. Make sure your evidence supports your thesis.

5. Content is important, but so is how you present your argument. Pay attention to grammar, diction, syntax, and penmanship. Avoid verbosity. Get to the point. Remember the KISS principle—Keep It Simple Scholar.

6. Although essays come in many shapes and sizes, a traditional format is the five-paragraph essay. Each paragraph usually has five sentences.

Now that you know all the components necessary for writing an essay, complete Activity 7.4. Remember, practice makes permanent.

[Paragraph 1: Thesis paragraph. This is the most important part of the essay. It establishes the argument and tone of what is to follow. It also is the first impression you make with your reader. You want to encourage your audience to continue to read. This paragraph should be a mini-essay. Think of it as an inverted triangle (refer back to Exhibit 7.3).

- Start by identifying the broad context (or setting) of the subject at hand.
- Next, present the arguments (the standards or categories) you will be considering in the essay. These must support your thesis.
- Finally, state your thesis. What is the main point? What will you try to prove in your essay?

The thesis should be clear, focused, and specific!]

When the colonists finally defeated the English in 1783, celebrations took place from Massachusetts to Georgia. Eight years of sacrifice and bloodshed were over. The colonists were independent. Quickly, however, this elation gave way to more serious concerns. The colonists had to build a national government. The nature and shape of this government were still a question. Now that independence had been achieved, the new nation was no longer an official part of the British economic system. The United States had to develop its own economic base. And the newly independent country had to establish its own cultural identity. That is, "What did it mean to be an American?" In effect, although independence had been achieved on the battlefield, political autonomy, economic independence and a distinct cultural cohesiveness were not foregone conclusions. The leaders of our nation had monumental tasks ahead of them.

[Transition sentence leading to next paragraph]

[Paragraph 2: Supporting evidence. Make sure your second paragraph begins with a *topic sentence*. Although this sentence may introduce the paragraph, it can appear anywhere. Usually you want it as close to the beginning as possible. Let the reader know immediately what you are proving in the paragraph. The rest of the sentences should *relate* to the topic sentence. The entire paragraph should support your thesis. You should include three to five substantial facts that *support the thesis*. Avoid irrelevant ("fluff") information. Stick to the topic.]

During the war, the thirteen states fought as a unit to defeat a common enemy. Maintaining this solidarity, however, was a major challenge for the first central government—The Articles of Confederation.

(continued)

exhibit 7.4 Continued.

[Transition. Following this transition, you should support the topic sentence with specific and substantial facts.]

[Paragraph 3: Supporting evidence. Use the same format as for Paragraph 2, but with a new category or area of argument. The topic sentence should set the tone for the paragraph.]

Although a rural-based economic system was in place, the United States had to develop its own industrial base as well as international markets.

[Once again, pertinent historical facts would need to follow this introduction.]

[Transition]

[Paragraph 4: Supporting evidence. Again, use the same format, but with a new category or area of argument. Here also the topic sentence should set the tone for the paragraph.]

While the nation's political and economic foundations received a lot of public attention and debate, the cultural identity of America was being more silently shaped. From art to literature to gender relationships, the American society established itself.

[Complete the paragraph with relevant support. Be specific with your information.]

[Transition]

[Paragraph 5: Conclusion. Tie the preceding four paragraphs together. Do not introduce new evidence or a new argument. Do, however, state the significance of your thesis and evidence. Reemphasize one or two key thesis words. That is, what is the connection to a larger body of knowledge? What are the implications of your argument? Avoid a simple summary. Make sure your reader understands the argument you just presented.]

The Revolutionary War established the United States of America as a free and independent nation. It also highlighted the many problems that had to be addressed by the young country. Winning independence was one thing—maintaining it was quite another. A system of government, an economic structure, and a cultural identity needed to be established. Success in these areas was necessary for the nation to prosper and progress.

THE FIVE-PARAGRAPH ESSAY   ACTIVITY 7.4

Develop a five-paragraph essay addressing a topic of your choice. Make an argument for your favorite music group; or explain why your parents should let you do something you really want to do; or tell your boss why you really deserve a raise; or tell the coach why you deserve to start the next game. Choose a topic for which you have a passion and develop a clearly supported argument. You can't become a better writer unless you practice. And it takes a lot of practice.

Paragraph 1:

_____

_____

_____

_____

Paragraph 2:

_____

_____

_____

_____

Paragraph 3:

_____

_____

_____

_____

Paragraph 4:

_____

_____

_____

_____

Paragraph 5:

_____

_____

_____

_____

What you've learned so far

Let's review what you've learned so far in this module.

1. Choose and focus on the topic:
   - Know the task you must accomplish.
   - Carefully read all the words.
   - Underline key words.

2. Develop a clear thesis statement:
   - Identify a topic.
   - Provide an opinion.
   - Structure your argument.

3. Choose supporting evidence:
   - Make sure your data support your thesis.
   - Try clustering.
     - Write a key word.
     - Ask yourself what other words come to mind.
     - Connect associations.

4. Organize your cluster notes:
   - Make a brief outline.
   - Establish how you will get from the beginning of your paper to the end in a logical manner.

5. Write:
   - Use the strategies you have learned to develop your argument.

6. Proofread, revise, and submit the final product.
   - Ask a friend to review your work. A second set of eyeballs may catch errors you have skipped over. Make corrections as needed.
   - Use the *Postwriting Essay Assessment* form in Activity 7.5 to evaluate your paper.
   - Submit the final draft at the appropriate time (end of the class period or the date on which the essay is due).

The length of time you spend on each step will vary according to the actual assignment. You will tackle an in-class essay a bit differently than you will a long-term homework project. And the writing skills you develop for the shorter essays will serve you well when it comes time for a lengthier research paper.

Exhibit 7.5 provides one more way to view the steps to writing an effective essay.

Evaluating it: How do you know if you have written an acceptable essay?

Use the checklist in Activity 7.5 to assess the quality of your essay. The successful student does not hand in an assignment just to turn something in. It should be reflective of thought and diligence.

POSTWRITING ESSAY ASSESSMENT: A CHECKLIST   ACTIVITY 7.5

○ 1. Did you correctly interpret the instructions? Did you understand each key word in the prompt?

○ 2. Is there a clearly stated thesis (main idea)?

   ○ A. Is there a topic?

   ○ B. Is an opinion presented?

   ○ C. Did you present a brief "road map" of how you will prove your argument?

○ 3. Is all of your support relevant to the topic and the opinion? Always ask, "Why is this fact or paragraph important? How does it support my thesis?"

○ 4. Is your evidence based on support, or is the essay full of unsubstantiated glittering generalities? For instance, don't say, "The government was in lots of trouble." Rather, be more specific and state, "The central government was weak because it lacked the power to tax and control commerce."

○ 5. Does the essay follow the sequence you established in your first-paragraph road map?

○ 6. Have you checked your grammar and sentence structure? Do subjects and verbs agree? Are you using the correct words to express your thoughts?

○ 7. Is your writing style and wording appropriate for your audience? As a rule, most school assignments should not use slang.

○ 8. Is the essay neat (penmanship, typing format, errors neatly corrected)?

○ 9. Have you read your paper aloud? Do this now—and *listen* to the words and sentences. Do they flow? Do they make sense? (This can be an eye-opening experience!)

○ 10. Is your name on the paper?

exhibit 7.5   The steps to writing effectively.

```
                    WRITING EFFECTIVELY
```

The Prompt
1. Understanding
2. "Mark up"

Your Decisions
1. Topic
2. Opinion
3. Evidence
4. Audience
5. Organization
6. Proofreading

Quick Outline
1. Clustering evidence
2. Thesis

5 X 5
1. Telling and showing
2. Writer's block?

Asking reporter questions
Who? What? When?
Where? Why? How?

Effective Communication Case Study 4

APPLYING YOUR SKILLS TO THE WORKPLACE

SITUATION. Omar is an office manager for a local insurance company. He has held the position for two years and received favorable job evaluations from his supervisor. Unfortunately, he has not seen an increase in salary.

"I'd like to give you a raise, Omar," says his boss, Mr. Dithers, at his annual evaluation. "But times are tough for everyone right now. Hang in there!"

"Nice words," thinks Omar, "but they don't put money in my pocket. I'm not keeping pace with inflation."

Omar likes his job, his coworkers, and his boss. However, there isn't much money left at the end of each month. Omar doesn't believe Mr. Dithers realizes just how valuable he is to the company. He's working as diligently as he knows how. But, with two kids to raise and night classes, even if he could put in more hours to earn extra money, he just doesn't have the time.

On his way to night class, Omar ponders the situation. He decides he's going to ask for a raise, but he just doesn't know how.

YOUR PROPOSED SOLUTION. What do you think Omar should do? Should he ask for a raise, or will that just make his boss angry? Does Omar have an inflated view of himself? Should he look for another job that pays more? Should he give his boss an ultimatum—"Pay me more or I'll have to resign."

PROPOSED SOLUTION. Later that evening, before his English composition class at City College, Omar buys a cup of coffee and formulates a plan of action.

Stop.   When he thinks calmly about the matter, Omar realizes that his boss does appreciate him. Mr. Dithers includes him on many important decisions, occasionally takes him to the country club for lunch, and generally is very respectful.

That is not the problem. The issue for Omar is to get a wage he believes complements his productivity.

Alternatives.   Omar writes down three choices:

"First, I could walk into Mr. Dithers's office and present an ultimatum: 'Give me a raise or I'll have to quit.'"

"Second, I could say nothing and continue to work as I have been and tighten my budget belt a little more."

"Third, I could present Mr. Dithers with a well-reasoned case as to why I deserve a raise."

Consequences.   Omar doesn't particularly like the confrontational nature of option number one. In addition, if there truly were no money for raises, he would be backing himself into a corner. He likes his job and coworkers, so he doesn't really want to quit.

Option two is the path of least resistance but he believes too strongly in this issue to pretend it doesn't matter.

The third choice allows him to express his reasoning in a calm and rational manner.

Selection.   Knowing that Mr. Dithers *always* respects a well-reasoned argument, Omar decides on the third option. And it will be a great time to use the persuasive writing techniques he is learning in class!

Implementation.   During the weekend, Omar drafts a memo to Mr. Dithers following the 5×5 method of writing. His introductory paragraph sets the stage for his main argument: *I respectfully request a pay raise.* This then leads to paragraphs two, three, and four, which provide specific reasons why he deserves a raise.

Paragraph two provides evidence of how he is a self-starter in the office. He needs very little supervision, and if he doesn't have a project, he starts one on his own.

Paragraph three details his strong work ethic. He arrives at work early and doesn't mind working late if a project needs a last-minute push. In fact, by doing extra work the funds budgeted to hire temporary help don't get spent. This saves the company money.

Paragraph four lists his cost-saving initiatives in the office.

The final paragraph is a clincher that reemphasizes his respect for Mr. Dithers and how they both shared the same visions for the growth of the company.

Pause.   Omar delivers the memo to Mr. Dithers's secretary and sets up an appointment for the next afternoon.

YOUR REACTION TO THE PROPOSED SOLUTION. Did Omar do the right thing? What do you think Mr. Dithers's reaction will be? What other options did Omar have? What is your evaluation of Omar's memo?

SUCCESS
STRATEGY

RESEARCH AND THE LIBRARY

Writing a research paper

Research papers serve various purposes. They provide practice in gathering, organizing, and presenting written information. They also allow a student to gain a more in-depth understanding of a particular topic. Some papers, usually term papers, require the student to *explain* or *describe* a particular topic. Others require the student to actually develop a thesis on an issue and present an argument supporting that particular view. Whatever the thrust of the assignment, you will need to gather source material from the "experts" on your topic.

Once you get over the initial shock of having to prepare a major research paper, it's time to get started. Here are a few basic ideas to keep in mind:

- What are your instructor's directions? Follow them *exactly*. Do not get creative with someone else's instructions. This would include the number of sources required, mechanics of the final product (typed, double-spaced, footnotes or endnotes, bibliographic style), and number of pages.

- When is this project due? Circle the date on your long-range planning calendar. Establish a schedule and follow it. The checklist in Activity 7.6 will help you.

Help! I don't know what to write about!

In most instances, the instructor will give you a broad topic about which to write. Your immediate task will be to narrow the focus of your research. A typical, and understandable, problem most students have is choosing a subject that is far too broad.

If your English instructor assigned a 7- to 10-page paper on the general topic of *nineteenth-century writers*, what would you do? (Panic is *not* an option!) Well, your first task would be to narrow the topic. What nineteenth-century writers would you research? Remember, it's a brief paper, so writing about the major themes of all European and American writers might be a bit ambitious.

Maybe you decide to write on nineteenth-century *American* writers. Good start, but this is still too broad. How about writers of the *late* nineteenth century? Well, that's better but still needs more focus. After all, do you really want to write about *every* late-nineteenth-century American writer? By process of elimination, you get to the point where you will concentrate on *one* writer—Mark Twain. Why did you pick Twain? Hopefully, it's because you find him interesting. (When possible, pick a topic that will be exciting to you. You have to live with it.)

But wait. Before you go running off in search of books on Huck Finn's creator, you have a bit more work to do. What about Twain are you going to research? His childhood? His early writing influences? His literary successes? His failures? His critics? In other words, you might wish to limit your research to one aspect of his career.

Once you have sufficiently narrowed the topic—the literary style of *Huckleberry Finn*—determine what you will prove. This becomes your central reason for researching and writing. Start with a question: "Why has *Huckleberry Finn* been a literary success?" Answer the question: "*Huckleberry Finn* has been critically acclaimed because it was written in an idiomatic style that *showed*, rather than merely *described*, what life on the Mississippi was like." This is the thesis you will need to prove in your paper.

Take a few minutes now to complete Activity 7.7.

ORGANIZING A SCHEDULE FOR YOUR RESEARCH PAPER   ACTIVITY **7.6**

○ Decide on your topic area and your approach to the topic. Probably the most vital task you will have early in your research is to narrow the focus of your topic.

○ Develop a *temporary* thesis. It's okay to revise as you gather data.

○ Determine what references you will use. Will you use the library or the Internet, or both?

○ Based on your initial research, develop an outline. Do you need to revise your thesis?

○ Conduct more research.

○ Write the first draft.

○ Proofread. Get a friend to read it also. Revise.

○ Write the second draft.

○ Proofread and revise.

○ Complete and submit the final copy *on time*. In fact, get it done early. Remember the "glitch factor" (see Module 4)?

There are two keys to successful completion of your paper:

1. focusing on your thesis
2. managing your time

Remember, the assignment is not going "to go away." You have to do it. So, make it easy on yourself and break all of the tasks into bite-sized and manageable chunks.

NARROWING THE FOCUS OF YOUR RESEARCH   ACTIVITY **7.7**

Choose a topic you find interesting. Now ask yourself, "Is this topic too broad? Can I narrow it any further? Can I find enough information on this topic? Will I have too much information with which to work?" Jot down your thoughts below.

_____

_____

_____

_____

_____

_____

How do I prove my opinion?

When confronted with a vast array of material, one can be easily over-whelmed. Try the following strategy once you have narrowed your topic and identified your thesis.[2]

To prove your opinion, establish a separate list for each of the following: people, events, issues, quotes, and places. For example,

- What are the names of the critics and experts who support your thesis?
- Is there an event that supports your thesis?
- Are there any pertinent issues that are clearly connected to this thesis?
- Are there any quotes that can add energy and support to your paper? A well-phrased quote about your topic can add the weight of an expert. A word of caution: Quotes should be short and sparing. Remember, the purpose of the paper is to get *your* thoughts on paper. You are not being asked to write a string of quotations. Be careful in this area.
- Would a reference to a particular place (geographic location) be helpful to your argument? If so, include it.

How do I gather my evidence?

A common misconception is that you should be able to sit down and pick a narrowly focused subject with little or no effort. If you have ever grappled with this task, you know it is not that simple. To come up with a reasonable topic you must do some initial research. Before you can engage in narrowing a topic, you have to know something about it.

Start by looking at your class notes, class textbooks (table of contents and bibliography), magazines, general and subject-specific encyclopedias, and related books. Take some initial notes. Develop a "flavor" for the topic. More than likely, you will need to make a trip to that formidable building on campus—the library. The research librarian is a vital tool for your search. You can also browse the Internet. Be aware, though, that if you don't have a narrowed topic, this can prove to be time-consuming (and even time wasting)—there is a vast amount of information on the Internet.

Narrowing your research topic

Here is a true story. A student was assigned a 10-page research paper for a United States History class. The task: "Pick any topic in post-1865 American History and develop a research paper."

Wow! Talk about broad. Although students may dislike rigid guidelines, there is something to be said for the structure such requirements provide. This assignment was challenging due to the vast array of topics the student could choose.

After some initial discussion, he decided to focus on the late nineteenth century (1880s–1890s). Now what? Where would *you* go to get your initial topic? What would *you* use to "jump-start" your writing battery?

---

[2]For a clear and simple organizing tool, I recommend Michael Edmondson, "The History Paper, Part III," *OAH Magazine of History,* Fall 1995, 31–35.

Well, this student decided to use what he had on hand—his class textbook. He reviewed the table of contents, chapter headings, and time lines. He wanted to pursue broad themes. This was a start, but he was still not sure what to do. So, he decided to brainstorm on paper.

Across the top of a piece of notebook paper, he wrote the following broad areas: Politics, Economics, Social, and Culture. From here, with the help of class notes and the text, and in no particular order, he listed historical concepts and events. All the student wanted to do at this stage was get something on paper—write now; choose later. Exhibit 7.6 shows what his listing looked like.

The student now had something to work with. His next step was to choose one of the topics. After doing a little reading, he settled on immigrants.

What do you think the next step was? What would you do?

Well, he had to narrow the focus. *What* about immigrants would he research? He came up with several choices:

- New Immigrants versus Old Immigrants: Why did the nations of origin start to change?
- Discrimination: What form(s) did discrimination take? Why did it exist? Was it more perceived than reality?
- Occupations: What industries attracted specific immigrant groups? Why?
- Residential patterns: Where did the immigrants live? Why? Did they mingle with other immigrant groups? Why or why not?

Eventually, the student decided to tackle the topic of occupations. He had developed a guiding question for his research. And remember, as you do your research, be flexible. You may need to make an adjustment, based on your findings, and move in a *slightly* different direction than originally thought.

The key: Do enough initial research so that you can make an intelligent decision on which topic and question to focus on. If you don't, you will end up wasting lots of valuable time and creating undue stress for yourself.

Student listing of possible topics.

exhibit 7.6

POLITICS	ECONOMICS	SOCIAL	CULTURE
Elections	Distribution of wealth	Class development	High culture
1896	Rise of corporation	Immigrants	Low culture
Military and mobilizing for war	Robber barons or captains of industry	Good	Parks
Suffrage	Labor unions	Bad	B-ball
Isolation vs. globalism	Gilded age	Alger Hiss and American dream	Saloons
Monroe Doctrine: evolution			Public school
Reform and scandals			

Help! I'm lost in the library and I can't get out!

It is not my intent to provide an exhaustive review of how to use the library. Many excellent courses and books[3] are already available on the topic. Your instructors can direct you to appropriate sources.

Let's briefly examine some of the basics to help with your library search. I suggest a library tour to familiarize yourself with the workings of the facility you will be using. I have never met a librarian unwilling to help a student.

In fact, get to know the reference librarian as soon as you can. This individual can save you a lot of wasted steps and worry. He or she will not, and should not, do your research, but he or she has the hands-on knowledge of sources of particular help in your field.

Every school library will have an electronic catalog of holdings. This is a listing of books and other resources in the library. Think of this as the table of contents for your library. It is your guide to volumes of information. You may even be able to access some or all of these files from your home personal computer. A call to your local library will provide that information.

The electronic catalog allows you to search your topic by author, title, subject, or keyword. An opening screen[4] might show something like this:

a = author

t = title

s = subject

tj = periodical title

k = keyword search

At this point, you would type in your choice. For example, for our nineteenth-century writer topic, you could type in any of the following:

a = twain, mark

t = huckleberry finn

s = 19th century writers

k = twain and criticism

If there is a match in the catalog, the next screen will present any number of choices on the subject you typed in on the previous screen. Follow the instructions at the bottom of the screen. Generally, if you type the number beside one of the items on the screen you will see an expanded view of the holding on the screen. This and subsequent screens usually present the following information:

1. author's name
2. title of work
3. publication information
4. physical description of the book (number of pages, illustrations, index)
5. International Standard Book Number (ISBN)

---

[3]One such resource is Jean Key Gates, *Guide to the Use of Libraries and Information Sources,* 7th ed. (New York: McGraw-Hill, 1994).

[4]For instance, LUIS (Library User Information System) is the electronic catalog used for the State of Florida's public universities.

6. general subjects to which this book applies (this can be of help in locating other material on your topic)

7. call number (needed to locate the book on the library shelf/stack)

8. status (is the book checked out or on the shelf?)

Follow command choices at the bottom of the screen to move forward or backward among the catalog choices. With just a little practice, you will be able to quickly navigate and access this valuable information from the computer terminal.

With command of the electronic card catalog, you will be able to access other forms of information, electronic or otherwise. You might wish to look at subject-specific indexes such as *American Writers* or *Contemporary Literary Criticism*. Sources such as *ERIC (Educational Resource Information Center)* provide a wide range of articles on varying topics in the educational field, for instance. This source, whether used in electronic form or in the older book-bound fashion, provides abstracts of articles. Other indexes provide synoptic views of longer articles. As a researcher, the abstract gives you a quick overview of the source and whether or not it is of use to your particular project.

If your library doesn't have an electronic card catalog, use the book-bound version of the *Readers' Guide to Periodical Literature* to find magazine and journal articles of interest. Newspapers, such as the *New York Times,* also have their own indexes.

There is a wealth of information in the library—but it won't do you any good if it remains on the shelf. Research is like putting a puzzle together. You have to search patiently for the correct pieces. Once the information is found, you must know what to do with it.

How do I know what stuff is important?

SUCCESS STRATEGY

Once you have narrowly defined your topic and started to take notes from your source material, the answer to this question will become more readily apparent. Earlier, I suggested that as you write a paragraph to ask yourself how it connects to your thesis. Apply this same principle to your term paper. If you wish to prove that Twain's style created his success, then you should focus on commentary about his literary skills. Why not see what the experts in the field have to say about the subject? An excellent source is the *Book Review Digest.* The *Digest* provides excerpts from full-length book reviews, complete with analysis and bibliographic citations to find the original review. Other literary digests or indexes will also help you see the main point of the topic.

How do I know if an Internet site is "good"?

The Internet has opened up a vast number of sources to us. It allows us to put our fingers instantaneously on a wide variety of information. It is quick, dynamic, and convenient. It also can provide us with incorrect or "bad" information.

Many people believe that if something appears on their computer screen it has to be the absolute truth. Not so. Let's turn now to Activity 7.8, which will help you to evaluate a website.

ACTIVITY 7.8 EVALUATING A WEBSITE

The purpose of this website evaluation is to get you to go to an Internet site, thoroughly review it, and then submit a report on that site. For this activity, find a website that addresses a *career area* you have (or think you may have) some interest in pursuing. Besides getting a chance to practice website evaluation techniques, this is an opportunity to research a workforce area in which you intend to make a living.

Answer the following questions:

1. What is the common name of the site? This is usually found on the home page.

2. What is the exact URL of the site? This is the address/location of the site. It will typically begin with http:// or http://www. *Note:* When typing in a URL be sure to type it exactly as it appears. If only one character is incorrect, the site will not be located.

3. Who is the author of the site? What are the credentials of the author? Include any affiliations (for example, university professor, government agency). If none are listed, state that. What evidence exists that the author(s) is qualified to publish this material? What is your opinion of the credentials of this author? If no credentials are listed, what conclusions can you draw from that? Do you "trust" this site? (Your answer can be stated in two or three sentences.)

4. Is the material accurately presented? Biased? Why? How might you determine the accuracy of this site? (Your answer can be stated in two or three sentences.)

5. Explore some of the hot links of this site. A hot link is a link that takes you immediately to another page or place on the same page simply by clicking your mouse button. What types of links are there? Specifically discuss one of these links. (Your answer can be stated in a couple of sentences.)

EVALUATING A WEBSITE, continued   ACTIVITY **7.8**

6. Would you recommend this site to other people? Why or why not? (Your
   answer can be stated in two or three sentences.)

   _____

   _____

   _____

7. Briefly, summarize what you learned from this site. Did you learn any
   new information? Did this site reinforce what you already knew? (Your
   summary can be stated in two or three sentences.)

   _____

   _____

   _____

A QUICK REVIEW

This module provided basic strategies for clear essay writing and basic tips
for surviving a research paper.

There are, really, only three ways to become a better writer—practice,
practice, and more practice. More specifically, the proficient writer

- knows the purpose of the writing assignment.
- takes time to plan an appropriate response.
- establishes an opinion that relates to the topic.
- provides evidence that supports the opinion.
- does not give up when he or she encounters writer's block.
- takes time to evaluate his or her work.
- has an organized schedule to complete research papers.
- effectively narrows the focus of a research topic to a workable proposition.
- is familiar with library resources (print, electronic, and human).

Take a few minutes now to review Exhibits 7.7 and 7.8.

exhibit 7.7   Some possible correlations with your learning style.

TOPIC	AUDITORY	KINESTHETIC	VISUAL
Analyzing the prompt	Physically mark up the prompt; orally dissect the prompt.	Physically mark up the prompt.	Physically mark up the prompt.
Organizing a paper/essay	Do a traditional outline with pen and paper; use a tape recorder.	When composing your ideas, try walking around the room as you think; manipulate pen and index cards.	Do a traditional outline with pen and paper; try to "see" the outline of material as it is developing in your mind; use "chunking" and cluster notes.
Writer's block	Turn on a tape recorder and say what comes to mind (stream of consciousness); brainstorm with a buddy.	Move about; manipulate index cards; use cut-n-paste.	Use stream-of-consciousness writing.
The library	Read appropriate handouts; get a supplemental book on using the library.	Physically tour the facility; manipulate the electronic catalogs.	Practice with electronic catalogs; access online catalogs.

exhibit 7.8   How to complement selected intelligences.

WHEN GIVEN AN ASSIGNMENT OR TASK, IF YOU ARE STRONG IN . . .	THEN ASK YOURSELF . . .
Logical-mathematical intelligence/5 x 5	"How can I use my abilities to see shapes and patterns to create a sound essay?"
Musical intelligence/ research paper	"How can I use my musical intelligence to narrow a research topic focus?"
Musical intelligence/ Internet sites	"How can I use this ability to find an interesting and credible site on the World Wide Web?"

Here are some things you can do to improve your learning environment:

- Make sure your personal study space is appropriate.
- Write at a time of day when your energies are highest.

Complete the following exercises.

1. Evaluate La Rochefoucauld's quote at the beginning of this module.

   _____

   _____

   _____

2. When evaluating an essay you have written, ask all of the following _except_
   A. Does my buddy like it?
   B. Is all of the evidence relevant to the topic?
   C. Does the essay follow the sequence established in the first paragraph?
   D. Is the writing appropriate for the intended audience?

3. The two keys to a successful research paper are
   A. a good computer and a broad topic.
   B. properly managed time and a good computer dictionary and grammar check.
   C. a broad topic and properly managed time.
   D. a focused topic and managed time.

4. When using an electronic library catalog, "tj" stands for
   A. periodical title.
   B. just the title.
   C. title juxtaposition.
   D. type of journal.

5. Which of the following are _basic_ decisions a writer must make?
   A. what topic
   B. what evidence
   C. what audience
   D. all of these

6. List three questions you can use to "jump-start" your "writing battery":
   A. _____
   B. _____
   C. _____

7. What does the acronym T.O.E.S. stand for?

   _____

   _____

8. Match the word to the proper definition:

   A. classify

   B. contrast

   C. describe

   D. evaluate

   E. relative importance

   _____ to explain an event, issue, topic

   _____ how two or more factors compare to one another

   _____ to provide differences

   _____ to judge, criticize, establish standards

   _____ to put things into categories

Checklist

Checklist of Selected Tips and Strategies

As a last review, collaborate with a classmate and write a brief description of how each of the following will help you become a more successful student.

WRITING STRATEGIES

1. Establishing a purpose

   _____

   _____

   _____

2. Reading instructions aloud

   _____

   _____

   _____

3. Analyzing the prompt

   _____

   _____

   _____

4. Making basic decisions

   _____

   _____

   _____

5. Planning a response

   _____

   _____

   _____

6. Looking at your T.O.E.S.

   _____

   _____

   _____

7. Implementing the 5×5 principle

   _____

   _____

   _____

8. Keeping to the point

_____

_____

_____

9. Using clustering

_____

_____

_____

10. Jump-starting your writing battery

_____

_____

_____

11. Understanding why the topic/opinion is important

_____

_____

_____

12. Knowing key words

_____

_____

_____

13. Making a plan

_____

_____

_____

14. Taking the Postwriting Essay Assessment

_____

_____

_____

15. Organizing for a research paper

_____

_____

_____

16. Narrowing a topic

_____

_____

_____

Whatshisname scheduled a whatchamacallit for when?

"A retentive memory is a good thing, but the ability to forget is the true token of greatness."

—ELBERT HUBBARD, NINETEENTH-CENTURY U.S. EDITOR, PUBLISHER, AND AUTHOR

"Many a man fails to become a thinker only because his memory is too good."

—NIETZCHE, NINETEENTH-CENTURY GERMAN-SWISS PHILOSOPHER

MODULE 8

Overview of This Module

WHY DO WE FORGET?

Know what you *can* forget

SUCCESS STRATEGY

The quotes at the beginning of this module might sound confusing; they seem out of place. Can a good memory actually have a downside?

You encounter an overwhelming amount of data each day of your life. Your mind already performs a function that successful students have learned to use for their benefit: *selective forgetting.* In their book, *Rapid Memory in 7 Days,* Joan Minninger and Eleanor Dugan briefly state, "Bright people remember less than average people because they drop out all the small stuff. They can focus their energy on important things instead of trivia."[1]

To cope with the vast quantities of information vying for your attention, you must learn to focus on only those things you wish. You must have a

---

[1]Joan Minninger and Eleanor Dugan, *Rapid Memory in 7 Days: The Quick-and-Easy Guide to Better Remembering* (New York: Berkeley Publishing Group, 1994), 17.

desire to retain information. No desire, no understanding, no memory! You also need to develop observational and listening skills. This requires discipline and concentration.

Finally, memory is the process of storing and finding information in the brain. You have to develop an efficient system for filing and retrieving that information. If you have been following the organizational strategies in these modules, you are well on your way to establishing effective recall strategies.

Let's start with a little demonstration. Without looking, picture the area to the left of where you are sitting. Describe what you see. Be specific. If there is a bookshelf, don't just say there are books on the shelf. In what order do they appear? What are the topics? What color are the books? Hardcover or soft cover? Now mentally look to your right. What kind of furniture is there? Colors? Fabrics? Designs? Length and width?

Think of the last meal you ate with someone. Who was at the table with you? *Exactly* where did these people sit? What were the people wearing? Colors? Styles? Leather, cotton, knit, suede? Socks? Canvas shoes or no shoes?

First, you must notice

If you are like most people, you probably couldn't answer many of these questions. Why not? More than likely, you did not *notice* the items. They were not important to you. Before anyone can learn anything, the material must be noticed.

Why do you forget?

Forgetting is the failure of a previously *learned* behavior to appear. If you haven't learned it, you can't possibly forget it!

We forget for a variety of reasons, either singly or combined:

- We fail to use what we have learned.
- The reward we received for learning is no longer present.
- A previously learned behavior interferes with a newly learned behavior.
- A newly learned behavior interferes with a previously learned behavior.
- The situation in which the new behavior must occur is different from the one in which the behavior was learned.

Let's develop this list a little further.

Memory blocks

It has happened to all of us at one time or another. We know the material, but we freeze on the exam or during the presentation. Why?

Emotional memory blocks. Ever since you can remember, you have struggled in your math classes. No matter what you seem to do, your grades are less than satisfactory. As you prepare for the first math exam of the term, you do not expect to do any better. Whether it is a fear of failure or the memory of some distressing prior experience, some of us are afraid of the challenges that wait inside the classroom door.

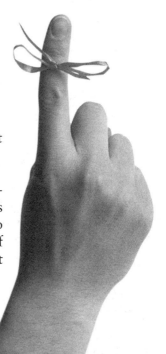

Physical memory blocks. You pull an "all-nighter" studying for the exam. You review everything that the instructor could possibly ask. You get to class feeling prepared for anything and suddenly all the information stored in your brain is a jumbled mess. You are so tired you can't think straight. So much for your hours of studying.

Mechanical blocks. You put a lot of time into your studies but you can't seem to recall the data during the exam. This is usually an indication of some retrieval difficulty. The "file cabinet" in your brain holds the information; however, you just threw the information into the drawers without labeling. Now you can't find what you need.

The brain's attic

You have a short-term and a long-term memory. The short term can last anywhere from 30 seconds to a couple of days. If the information is not used, it is virtually lost to you.

The long-term memory consists of those items that have not been "lost." For whatever reason—practice, concentration, desire—you have retained these data. "But," you reasonably may ask, "why do I still forget things when it comes to test time? I've practiced. I have desire. But my test grades sure don't reflect this!"

Retrieval failure—and what you can do about it

One point that has been repeated is your need for desire. Let's add something to this equation.

desire + effective retrieval strategies = memory

Sounds rather simplistic, doesn't it? But there are a number of obstacles to overcome before you can achieve a more uninhibited retrieval.

SUCCESS STRATEGY

Poor labeling. The better your filing system, the better your ability to find the data you are looking for. Think of your brain as a filing cabinet. Organize the "cabinet." Label the drawers, the files, and the folders. When you learn a new piece of information, place it in the proper file folder. Now you know where it is, and you'll be able to retrieve it when you need it.

What would happen if you just threw pieces of paper into the file cabinet drawer without any order whatsoever? Obviously you would have a difficult time finding material. Yet, this is what a lot of us do with vital information. Just as you would store valuables carefully, do the same with the facts, concepts, and generalizations with which you come into contact. Remember the suggestion to review your notes nightly? The 3Rs (review, relate, reorganize) will help you file. Developing connections is the best way to fight against improper filing.

Disuse. Just like with your muscles, if you don't use information, you will, more than likely, lose it. Ever have difficulty remembering some course material after a prolonged vacation from school? The reason is simple—you have not used the information. Once you start using the information again, your memory usually returns (assuming you have labeled the information correctly).

Extinction. Our schools are based on a series of rewards. These incentives vary, ranging from smiley faces to grades to awards for high GPA. Many of us have been conditioned by these extrinsic rewards—that is, those given to us by someone else. The grade, for instance, becomes the overriding reason for performance. Once the reward (grade) is removed, the incentive to continue to work with the material is removed. No reward, no effort, no retention.

There is a need, however, to develop intrinsic (internal) reasons to master your work.

Response competition. Visualize this scenario. You have studied for a science exam. Your science class is the last class of your school day, so before you get to this exam, you have to go through your English, history, and math classes. Each subject introduces you to more and more data. Your brain feels like it is going to burst! Welcome to the world of competing information. If you haven't developed a sound retrieval system, frustration is sure to set in.

Situational variation. Let's just call this stage fright. Consider these scenarios. You practiced that guitar lead for months. You never missed a lick. The first time you perform it in public—you guessed it—your fingers turn to jelly. Or you never flubbed a line during drama rehearsal. Opening night has arrived, and you can't remember your name! Why? The situation—the venue—has changed. You practiced in one environment but had to perform in quite a different situation. Practice the material in various situations to help eliminate a distraction.

Practice, as with the other topics discussed, is essential for retention. The graphs in Exhibit 8.1[2] provide a general view of the importance of reviewing (practicing) class material.

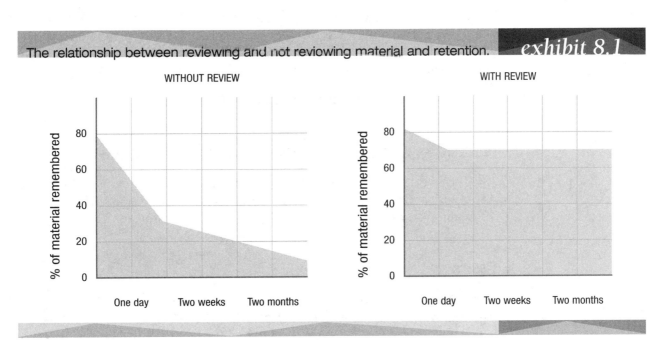

The relationship between reviewing and not reviewing material and retention.   *exhibit 8.1*

[2]Henry E. Florey, Jr., *Study Orientation Skills (Participant Manual)* (Tuscaloosa, AL: Author, 1987), 57.

Memory ≠ understanding

Before we move into specific strategies, let's set the record straight on one issue. While an effective memory may be impressive, and it may even help you get by on tests, it does not indicate that you understand the material. In fact, a "good memory" might end up being one of your (unknown) weaknesses. Sounds like a contradiction, doesn't it?

Some people are mechanical klutzes. If they had to, they could memorize the parts of a carburetor, but they wouldn't be able to explain their operation. Similarly, some students spend many hours in school memorizing lists of vocabulary words and spelling words. Then their exams and quizzes reflect high scores. But, in reality, the students could be missing out on the important rules that guide spelling exceptions. This, in turn, can cause a great deal of heartache and embarrassment in later years when they have to learn basic spelling rules they should have understood in elementary school.

SUCCESS STRATEGY

The problem: These students are more interested in receiving a great grade—the extrinsic motivator, but they really need to develop intrinsic rewards—and learn the basic relationships.

True learning will usually cause some frustration. After all, learning indicates a change in behavior. Learning to accommodate new methods and information can be rather disconcerting to some of us. So, too, with memory strategies. As you review the ideas in the next section, keep two points in mind. First, since you are not used to them, they will initially seem awkward. Don't give up for that reason alone. Second, not every technique is for you. Pick and choose—but find something that works for you.

Memory = the foundation

Before you can truly understand material, you need to develop your ability to retain and retrieve information. Once you have established this foundation, understanding the material—be it in the classroom, on your job, or in your hobby—will be close at hand.

desire + efficient filing + effective retrieval strategies = understanding

IT'S A MATTER OF FOCUSING ENERGIES

Have you ever been introduced to someone only to forget his or her name within two minutes? This can be embarrassing. How about dates and numbers? Or your reading assignment? What's a person to do?

Desire

Most people forget because *they choose not to remember.* It really is that straightforward. You must have the desire to understand in order to remember effectively. Concentration is the name of the game. Listening, for instance, is an activity that requires focus. I am not asking you to *hear;* I am asking you to *listen.*

Active listening = improved memory

Here is a multistep strategy to help you remember more of what you are *listening* to.

1. **Focus.** You need to pay attention to the speaker, whether he or she is your boss, your teacher, your friend, or your parent. People who *choose* not to concentrate should not complain when they can't remember a thing. Practice courtesy and you will retain more. Pay attention to the speaker. Put aside other distractions. Focus on the words and meanings.

2. **Find relevance.** Face it, not every teacher is going to be a living, breathing dynamo. Find something in the presentation and focus on it. Find a relationship to something you already know.

3. **Listen with your ears—not your mouth.** Too many people are busy mentally phrasing their response while the speaker is still speaking. You can't understand the speaker if you are just waiting to jump in and give your opinion. If you "listen" in this manner, you are creating your own distraction.

4. **Participate.** Once the speaker has finished, rephrase what was said. If you can explain, in your own words, what has just been presented, you will have a better chance of retention. By paraphrasing you are, in effect, rehearsing the new material. Practice leads to understanding.

5. **Ask questions.** This is also part of the class participation strategy. Ask for clarification, relationships, or the significance of the topic at hand. Not only are you drilling the information, but you are also doing it in the context of the big picture of the presentation. This will help in the development of memory hooks (discussed later).

6. **Offer another explanation or another application.** This is a particularly effective strategy in classes that follow a discussion or seminar-style format. As you process the new information, try to present another side of the issue. Do not do this in a combative manner; rather, attempt to understand other aspects of the topic. This allows for analysis and, consequently, better understanding.

The key to these steps is the desire to want to understand. By becoming actively involved, you will be more apt to retain the information.

Memory

APPLYING YOUR NEW SKILLS TO THE WORKPLACE

For this case study, you are given only the situation. You will supply a solution.

SITUATION. Joey will be graduating from the university at the end of this semester. In addition to being on the dean's list each of the last three semesters, he has engaged in a wide variety of extracurricular activities. During this last semester, he decides to attend as many job fairs as he can schedule. He prepares a brief and professional résumé, buys an appropriate suit, and trims his hair. He looks good and feels ready.

But after a few of these fairs, Joey realizes he has a problem he had not noticed before. Once he introduces himself to a company representative, his mind goes blank. Within moments, he forgets the person's name. He listens attentively and nods his head in agreement, picks up brochures, and then moves to the next table. There he repeats the same process.

After a few of these events, he notices that it is not unusual to run into some of the same representatives at other job fairs. When they wave to him in recognition, he is embarrassed because he does not remember their names or much about what they said to him at the last fair. This is starting to rattle his confidence.

In desperation, Joey comes to you, a valued friend, and seeks your advice.

YOUR REACTION AND PROPOSED SOLUTION. Why do you think Joey is having this difficulty? Is it possible a dean's list student can have a "bad" memory? Using the SAC-SIP method of problem solving, help Joey devise a plan.

Stop.

_____

_____

_____

Alternatives.

_____

_____

_____

Consequences.

_____

_____

_____

Selection.

_____

_____

_____

Implementation.

_____

_____

_____

Pause.

_____

_____

_____

YOUR REACTION. Why do you believe the plan you propose is the best for Joey? Are there any potential problems with this solution?

Retrieval

SUCCESS STRATEGY

It should be obvious by now that the topics of the preceding modules neatly tie into one another. For instance, if your retrieval problem stems from poor labeling (remember the file cabinet example), review the reading strategies presented in Module 6. Skimming, scanning, questioning, outlining, and anticipating make information processing more efficient. The more you review (study) the more likely you will be able to retain and retrieve.

"What about my class notes?" you may ask. "I can't seem to make any lasting sense of these scribblings." There are a couple of techniques you can employ here.

First, review the link between Modules 5 and 6, the classroom experience and reading strategies. Ask yourself, "What are the connections between my homework reading and the class presentations?" With a little practice, you will be able to determine these relationships easily. Once you establish them you will have an increased ability to retain, understand, and retrieve. This moves beyond shear memory. The material starts to take on a life of its own. It makes sense.

Another helpful technique is the data retrieval chart (DRC). It is an organizational model that has been used for many years in education. The model's abbreviated format allows the assimilation of vast quantities of data in an efficient manner. It is an excellent tool for establishing relationships. Not only can you use it to review your notes, but it is also a handy outline for organizing your reading assignments.

Students of varying levels have used the following examples. The model in Exhibit 8.2 was developed for students studying the American War for Independence. The DRC in Exhibit 8.3 was used to introduce college freshmen to a unit on the Middle Ages. The DRC in Exhibit 8.4 helped a college class compare and contrast the interaction of various minority groups in the United States. Finally, a student organized a reading assignment using Exhibit 8.5.

exhibit 8.2   A DRC for students studying the American War for Independence.

THE NEW COLONIAL SYSTEM

Prime Minister	British Action	Colonial Response
Grenville		
Rockingham		
Townshend (Pitt)		
North		

As you can see after studying Exhibits 8.2–8.5, the DRC can be used to compare authors, scientific findings, historical developments, artistic relationships, and the like. Each cell allows for easy comparison with another cell. Relationships, which are vital to improving your memory, are easily established.

Don't wait for the teacher to provide a DRC. Make up your own when reviewing and reorganizing your notes. This becomes a great one-page study guide—efficient, effective, and practical.

SUCCESS STRATEGY

Mental pictures

We have a tendency to think in pictures. We consciously try to put thoughts into images and then cluster these images into relationships. Clustering is a strategy we used with our writing to gather supporting evidence for a thesis (Module 7). Employ the same technique here—just do it with mental pictures.

For instance, refer to the DRC on "The New Colonial System" in Exhibit 8.2. Visualize the British in their red coats. See the Boston Tea Party in your mind. Imagine the first shots at Lexington and Concord. This sort of creativity uses much more of the brain than if you just attempted to memorize the words without a clear conception of what was actually transpiring. (For a more detailed explanation of this technique, you may wish to listen to Kevin Trudeau's *Mega Memory*[3] audiocassette on this topic.)

---

[3]Both Trudeau and Roger Swartz (1991) praise the power of mental pictures. Swartz believes we will have more efficient retention if we associate material with images that are "nonsensical, ridiculous, sensual, bizarre, colorful, and on a grand scale" (94–95).

exhibit 8.3

HEIRS OF THE ROMAN EMPIRE

Introduction: The Middle Ages is the term used for the (approximately) 900-year period from the political demise of Rome (fifth century) to the beginnings of Modern Times (approximately fourteenth to fifteenth century). Some historians refer to the Early Middle Ages as the Dark Ages (fifth to tenth century). It was characterized by general disorder, decline, and lack of appropriate administrative machinery. The Later Middle Ages (eleventh century to fourteenth/fifteenth century) was a period of more advancement. This period of history generally refers to the Western part of the European continent.

	Byzantine Empire	Islamic Empire	Germanic Kingdoms (Early)	Germanic Kingdoms (Late)
Administration				
Contributions				
Events of Significance				
Challenges				

Names

Remembering names does not have to be difficult. A few simple techniques will avoid embarrassment and impress people.

- *Decide you want to remember the name.* Make a conscious effort. Say to yourself, "I want to remember this person's name."
- *Listen and repeat.* Carefully listen to the name of the individual. Repeat it. Ask for a spelling of the name. Use the name immediately. An exchange might go something like this:

"Steve, I would like you to meet my friend Iggie."

"Iggie, I'm pleased to meet you. You know, Iggie is quite a unique name. I remember a rock group back in the 70s by the name of Iggie and the Stooges. That wasn't you by chance? Well, it was nice meeting you, Iggie. I look forward to talking with you later."

exhibit 8.4   A DRC for studying the interaction of minority groups in the United States.

MINORITY STATUS IN THE UNITED STATES

Minority groups have responded in different ways to dominant group reactions. Use this chart to organize your thoughts and analyze the evolution of dominant–minority interaction in the United States.

	African Americans	Mexicans	Native Americans	Puerto Ricans	Trends
How was minority status achieved?					
Structural factors that have affected the group					
Stereotypes					
Discrimination (examples):					
Adjustment patterns (e.g., assimilation)					
Primary issues relating to the group					
Relative deprivation? (yes/no/evidence)					
Trends					
What would the dominant group like to say to the minority group?					
What would the minority group like to say to the dominant group?					
What does the future hold?					
Your recommendations					

Of Mice and Men

John Steinbeck introduces a variety of characters in this classic novel. Use this chart to analyze the significance of each character to the overall story line.

Character	When introduced	Symbolism	Significance
George			
Lennie			
Slim			
Candy			
Crooks			
Carlson			
Curley			
Curley's wife			
Old dog			

In a matter of about 15 seconds, the new name was used five times. Practice makes permanent.

- *Look at the face.* Lock the name to the face.
- *Notice physical features.* Does this person possess any unique features? Very short, very tall, long hair, big nose, beautiful eyes, or lots of jewelry? Exaggerate this feature. Have fun with this! You will be sure to remember the name.

Mnemonics

This strange-looking word (knee-mon-icks) is a strategy to trick your mind. It allows you to play games. Let's look at four examples.

Acronyms. Most students have been introduced to these. An *acronym* is a word formed from the letters (usually the first letters) of other words.

Do you wish to remember the names of the Great Lakes? Just remember *H.O.M.E.S.* This stands for Huron, Ontario, Michigan, Erie, and Superior.

SUCCESS STRATEGY

Acrostics. An *acrostic* uses the first letter of each word to create a sequential message. Having trouble with the order of mathematical operations? Simple. *P.E.M.D.A.S. (Please Excuse My Dear Aunt Sally)*. Now you will forever remember to first do the operation in parentheses, followed by exponents, multiplication, division, addition, and subtraction.

Want to remember the notes assigned to the lines of a musical staff? *E.G.B.D.F. (Every Good Boy Does Fine)*.

How about the taxonomic levels in biology? *King Philip Came Over For Green Stamps (Kingdom, Phylum, Class, Order, Family, Genus, Specie)*.

The hook, number, or peg system.[4] Associate a number or objects with a concept you wish to remember. Create a vivid and outrageous picture of the peg and the concept. The more vivid the image, the more of your brain is engaged, and the better chance to retain and retrieve. For instance, one memory technique uses the following number–rhyme list for a peg system:

1. gun	6. pick
2. goo	7. heaven
3. knee	8. bait
4. roar	9. line
5. hive	10. pen

Let's now assume you need to remember this list of chores:

1. Clean your room.
2. Wash the dishes.
3. Feed the cats.
4. Write a thank-you note to your uncle.
5. Mow the lawn.
6. Set the table for dinner.
7. Take out the trash.
8. Do your homework.
9. Walk the dog.
10. Vacuum the rug.

Your next task is to associate each chore with the hook number/image. Create a picture that is crystal clear and vivid. Your associations between the peg list and the items you wish to remember could look like this:

1. A *gun* was held to my head until I *cleaned my room*.
2. I scrubbed and scoured all of the *goo* as *I washed the dishes*.
3. My bouncing *knee* seemed to be a comfortable place for the *cats to feed*.
4. I can just hear Uncle Bubba *roar* with laughter as he reads my *thank-you note*.
5. Bees swarmed from the *hive* when I unknowingly ran over it *while mowing the lawn*.

---

[4]This system is introduced in many study skills books and programs. Some use the same words, whereas others use variations, but the principle is the same. For further discussions, see Florey, 60; Minninger and Dugan, 86–87; and Matte and Henderson, 115–17.

6. Imagine the job it was to *pick up* each dish I shattered while *setting the table for dinner.*

7. *Heaven* is never having to *take out the trash.*

8. My instructors always *bait* me with an incentive to *do my homework.*

9. Staying in a straight *line* is very difficult when *walking my dog.*

10. I finally found my *pen* when I *vacuumed the rug.*

The associations do not have to be logical. All you are trying to do is create a picture of the item you need to remember. This system can work with lists, such as vocabulary words, bones of the body, and parts of speech. (A word of caution, though. You may remember the list, but that doesn't mean you understand the information. As with all the strategies in this book, pick the one that fits the situation you are facing.)

Linking.   Your instructor just told you to know the Bill of Rights (the first 10 amendments to the Constitution) by tomorrow. How would you accomplish this task? One way is to establish a story with the main points of each amendment. Once again, the more odd the picture, or image, or story, the better the chance of it sticking in your head. Here's one example.

> You can imagine the <u>expression</u> on my face when I saw the <u>armed</u> bear marching <u>troops into my house.</u> He wanted them to <u>search</u> the bathroom to make sure no one was there who might steal my <u>life, liberty, or property.</u> Just then, a <u>lawyer</u> ran into the house saying the troops must be given a <u>trial by a jury</u> of bears. The tooth fairy wanted to sentence the troops to dance with wolves but this was too <u>cruel and unusual a punishment.</u> The troops were glad to be in America, where they had many rights—<u>some written and some not.</u> The bear went to the Holiday Inn, where he had a <u>reservation</u> for the night.

The underlined phrases correspond to the amendments.

Sure, it's silly, but it just might be what sparks your memory. The key with linking is to establish a vivid mental picture of *relationships.* It might also make studying a bit more enjoyable. See what your imagination can do!

Practice

When trying to learn new material, you need to do three things: practice, practice, and practice some more. To learn a new skill you need to perform activities that stretch your mind. Just like an athlete does stretches, calisthenics, and wind sprints to get in shape, so do you need to do mental gymnastics. Consider your mental warm-ups as mind exercises. Use them and you will expand your capabilities.

A QUICK REVIEW

There are three steps to remembering information: noticing, storing, and retrieving.[5] You must see something, put it someplace, and then go find it. Use hooks and linkages.

There is a difference between memory and understanding. Memory allows for the retention and retrieval of material. Understanding takes you to a higher level.

---

[5]Minninger and Dugan, 27–41.

The key to comprehension is the creation of relationships. You must concentrate on the task at hand. No desire, no results. You must focus your energies on the

- reasons you forget—and find a solution.
- ability to identify the important information (remember the 80/20 principle).
- development of an efficient and effective filing system.
- skill of active listening.
- use of organizing models (DRC, mnemonics, mental imaging).

Whatever you learn, use the new knowledge as soon, and as often, as possible. Take a few minutes now to review Exhibits 8.6 and 8.7.

exhibit 8.6   Some possible correlations with your learning style.

TOPIC	AUDITORY	KINESTHETIC	VISUAL
Storage and retrieval	Use acronyms and acrostics; listen to tapes; actively listen and participate in class discussions; offer alternative explanations.	Construct a DRC; use a mental image of movement; watch a video; use flash cards.	Use mental imaging, flash cards, a DRC, or acronyms and acrostics.
Building vocabulary	Do crossword puzzles.	Play a game of Scrabble.	Play a game of Pictionary.

exhibit 8.7   How to complement selected intelligences.

WHEN GIVEN AN ASSIGNMENT OR TASK, IF YOU ARE STRONG IN . . .	THEN ASK YOURSELF . . .
Interpersonal intelligence/ finding relevance of material	"How can I use this ability to determine how various items are related?"
Spatial intelligence/DRCs	"How can I use this intelligence to construct a DRC?"
Intrapersonal intelligence/ participation	"How can I use my self-knowledge to participate in class?"

Here are some things you can do to improve your learning environment:

- Seat location in the classroom is critical; avoid putting yourself in a distracting place.
- Limit your intake of distracting stimuli.

Complete the following exercises.

1. Evaluate the opening quote by Nietzche.

   _____

   _____

   _____

2. List three reasons that explain why we forget:
   A. _____
   B. _____
   C. _____

3. Define "forgetting."

   _____

   _____

   _____

4. Match the term with the description:
   A. emotional memory block
   B. mechanical memory block
   C. physical memory block
   _____ when you are so tired you can't think straight
   _____ when fear of failure distresses you to the point you will not perform
   _____ when you have the answer on the tip of your tongue but just can't think of it

5. A(n) _____ is a word formed from the letters (usually the first) of other words.

6. A(n) _____ uses the first letter or letters of words to create a message that helps one remember some special sequence.

7. Name three mnemonic strategies to help you improve your retention and retrieval.
   A. _____
   B. _____
   C. _____

Checklist

Checklist of Selected Tips and Strategies

As a last review, collaborate with a classmate and write a brief description of how each of the following will help you become a more successful student.

MEMORY AND RELATIONSHIPS

1. Recognizing _why_ you forget

2. Learning how to forget

3. Labeling your "filing cabinet"

4. Understanding that if you don't use it you'll lose it

5. Learning that memory ≠ understanding

6. Understanding that frustration is okay

7. Focusing on the speaker: Active listening

8. Finding relevance: Active listening

9. Listening without speaking: Active listening

10. Participating: Active listening

11. Asking questions: Active listening

12. Applying the knowledge: Active listening

13. Connecting homework with class work

14. Using a DRC

15. Thinking in pictures

16. Finding a link for names

_____

_____

_____

17. Using acronyms

_____

_____

_____

18. Using acrostics

_____

_____

_____

19. Using hooks

_____

_____

_____

20. Using new knowledge as soon as possible

_____

_____

_____

TEST PREPARATION

*There's no business
like prep business*

"Every human mind is a great slumbering power until awakened by a keen desire and by definite resolution to do."

—EDGAR F. ROBERTS, WRITER

MODULE 9

Overview of This Module

BRINGING IT ALL TOGETHER

Test anxiety

Test anxiety or inefficient test-taking strategies?

Putting your study skills to work for you: Everything is connected

Competence + confidence = improved self-esteem

THE FINAL CHECKLIST

Successful students have a plan

Postexam analysis

Hey, isn't this where we started? Assessment of strengths and weaknesses

Emergency studying

Test-taking strategies

A QUICK REVIEW

BRINGING IT ALL TOGETHER

The preceding pages have presented an abundance of strategies. I would guess, however, you still have one question, "How does all of this help my GPA?" That is a fair question. Although grades are not the be all and end all of your school existence, they are important in our educational system.

A key point throughout the modules has been to develop understanding and relationships. Do this, and the grades *will* follow. Perhaps you remember the old adage, "Give a man a fish and you feed him for a meal. Teach him to fish and you feed him for a lifetime."

Well, these strategies are *self-generating*—not self-terminating. Learn and apply them and you will benefit for the rest of your life.

Test Anxiety

Test: A series of questions to determine one's knowledge

Anxiety: Distress, apprehension, worry

Test anxiety: The apprehension about one's ability to perform acceptably on a series of questions designed to determine one's knowledge

Why do students fear exams? After all, a test is only a piece of paper with words on it. This piece of paper cannot do harm to the student. But, the anxiety remains. Take a few minutes now to complete Activity 9.1, which will help you pinpoint your fears about taking exams.

WHY ARE YOU ANXIOUS ABOUT EXAMS?   ACTIVITY 9.1

Check any of the following thoughts that may cause, or have caused, you some
anxious moments on test day.

○ The instructor will be upset with a poor performance.

○ I'll be upset with a poor performance.

○ My parents will be upset with a poor performance.

○ I'll feel like a dummy if I don't do well.

○ A poor test grade will kill my GPA.

○ I mentally freeze.

○ My attitude is that tests are dumb anyway.

○ I know the material, but I freeze when I'm timed.

○ My mind drifts during the exam.

○ I tend to look at two or three test items at one time.

○ I suddenly realize I should have crammed the night before.

○ I speak to myself with a lot of negative self-talk (distortions).

○ I have so much nervous energy I cannot focus.

○ I don't have confidence in myself.

○ I always seem to score worse than I expect.

○ I fear what this exam will do to future opportunities (e.g., jobs).

○ Other people distract me with their movements.

○ I feel nauseous.

○ I feel tense from head to toe.

○ I do a lot of last-minute talking with friends about the exam.

○ Other reasons: _____

_____

_____

Now, look at the items you checked. Do you notice any similarities among
them? Closer inspection will reveal the following categories:

   (Y) how you view **y**ourself

   (O) how **o**thers perceive you

   (U) **u**nrealistic goals (is your "sky" too high?)

   (T) **t**hought distractions

   (U) for all your talk, you were just **u**nprepared

   Y.O.U.T.U. (YOU TOO) can conquer test anxiety.

SUCCESS STRATEGY

While the paper cannot harm you, your perception of the situation can lead you to uneasiness. It is a matter of attitude. If you lack confidence going into an exam your perception will become reality.

Let's look at some student-tested strategies and tips.

■ *Realistically evaluate the situation.* If you are panicky prior to exams, try this: Ask yourself, "What is the worst-case scenario? What is the very worst thing that can happen to me as a result of this exam?" Write this on a piece of paper. Now, objectively evaluate what you have written. Are there any distortions in your perceptions? That is, if you look at the situation realistically, what will *probably* happen? Once you have identified this, I want you to *visualize success.* What would you tell a friend who is nervous about an exam? I doubt you would tell your friend that he or she is stupid and destined to fail! Give yourself credit for what you know and what you can do.

■ *"Blocking" your test paper.* If your eyes tend to drift from one item to another during the exam, this technique will help you focus. You'll need two blank pieces of paper. Place one piece over the item above the one you are working on and the other on the succeeding item. For example, if you are working on problem three, "block out" two and four. You force your eyes to focus on only one item. (Always get your instructor's permission before using any additional pieces of paper during an exam.)

■ *Talk yourself through the exam.* If you can sit away from other students, it might be helpful to say quietly the test items aloud. Some of my students who have used this method believe it helps them calm down to "hear" the test.

■ *Remove yourself from distraction.* If possible, sit as far away from any distractions as possible. This means staying away from windows, open doors, noisy students, and the like.

■ *Become familiar with format.* Ask the instructor if he or she has past exam versions to review. By becoming familiar with the teacher's particular format, you are also mastering the content.

■ *Consider tutoring.* If you have been diligent with the content and assignments but still have difficulties with the subject matter, you may wish to seek additional help from the instructor or a student tutor. The campus dean or academic adviser should have information on peer tutors.

■ *Know your material.* Don't shortchange yourself. The more comfortable you are with the content, the more confident you will be on the exam. Follow the strategies in this book and there will be no reason to cram. Timely and organized studying will help you become comfortable, confident, and successful.

■ *Find out if "props" are allowed.* If you have a math test requiring many formulas, can you write each formula on an index card and use them during the exam? How about your notes? Will the instructor allow their use during the exam? (If so, hopefully you followed the note-taking strategies in Module 5.)

■ *Work with a timed situation.* Prior to exam day, practice putting yourself under pressure. Complete a specified number of items in a time frame that is roughly similar to an exam situation. If you can get an old exam from your instructor, complete it in the same amount of time you will have during the exam period. Become familiar, and comfortable, with the element of time.

■ *Ask your instructor about an alternative testing environment.* If distractions are really a problem, ask the instructor if you can complete the exam in an empty room if one is available.

Test anxiety or inefficient test-taking strategies?

Some students are not anxious about exams. They are prepared and comfortable come test day. But they still perform at a subpar level. The problem, in this case, may be one of time—they usually run out of it. If this is your problem, try the following suggestions.

Before you begin writing your exam answers, review all items. Get a "feel" for the test. How long will you need to do page one? Page two? In other words, establish a pace for yourself. Then proceed as follows:

SUCCESS STRATEGY

■ *Keep track of time.* Wear a watch. This is your responsibility.

■ *Do the easy items first.* If you do run out of time, you don't want to miss the easy points. "Easy" refers to content as well as item type. Obviously, make sure you answer all the questions you *know*. You may wish to do the item types you are most comfortable with before you tackle the more challenging ones. If matching is easy for you, do it first.

■ *Watch for trigger words.* Don't get an item wrong because you failed to see a trigger word. Underline, circle, and/or box key words. (Be sure you are allowed to write on the test paper.)

You can also prepare for content as well as the timed situation before exam day. Do as many practice tests as you can in a testlike environment. Depending on how much of a concern this is for you, you may give thought to doing a practice test in the actual classroom itself for a specified period of time. Ask your teacher.

Putting your study skills to work for you: Everything is connected

These modules have emphasized the need to relate information. You have learned strategies on various study skills topics.

Let's examine how the study skills strategies you have learned are related—and how they connect to test preparation. (We will be talking about test preparation for the classroom and teacher-made exams. Test preparation for exams such as the PSAT, SAT, ACT, or GRE involve other strategies that are not addressed here.)

A review of each of the steps to effective studying in Exhibit 9.1 looks like this:

■ *Goals.* Establish an attitude and know where you are going.

■ *Time management.* Establish your plan of how to get where you are going. Don't forget to tap into your learning style.

exhibit 9.1   The steps to effective studying.

Putting your study skills to work for you: Everything is connected.

GOALS

I will increase my science [history, English, math] grade by one letter grade by the end of the semester.

MEMORY
- Learn relationships.
- Connect everything.

TIME MANAGEMENT
- Use calendars and establish priorities.
- Complete homework.
- Review regularly—be sure to work with learning style.

TEST PREPARATION

WRITING STRATEGIES
- Choose a topic, state an opinion, and provide support for it.
- Use notes and reading.

CLASSROOM EXPERIENCE
- Implement the 3 Rs.

READING STRATEGIES
- Skim, scan, question, and read with a purpose.

- *Classroom experience.* Actively listen, review, reorganize, and relate.
- *Reading strategies.* Actively read with a purpose. Relate to the big picture of the classroom experience.
- *Writing strategies.* Do you know enough about the topic to state an opinion and support it?
- *Memory.* Obviously, if you can't retrieve the information it will be extremely difficult to perform well on an exam.

Utilizing these strategies will lead to test-taking success.

Competence + confidence = improved self-esteem

SUCCESS
STRATEGY

If you have diligently reviewed and practiced the study skill strategies found in these modules, you probably have noticed that each step along the way prepares for the exam. The arrows in Exhibit 9.1 indicate the continuous and flowing nature of these strategies. Once you understand and accept this fact, you are well on your way to becoming the successful student you have always wanted to be. No more cramming. Say good-bye to test anxiety. Welcome competence, confidence, and improved self-esteem.

This does not mean that you do not need to do some specific test preparation tasks immediately prior to the exam. You must consciously tie all of the material together so you can see the big picture. Test preparation is not a one-time event. It is a process.

THE FINAL CHECKLIST

When it comes to test taking, a positive mental attitude will carry you a long way. Sometimes it is a matter of semantics. I have had teachers tell me that their students go to pieces at the mention of a "test." But tell the students they are having a "quiz," an "exercise," a "worksheet," or an "opportunity," and the anxiety is relieved immediately. If that works for you, then use it. The point here is not to be caught up in words. *Visualize* success—and then *achieve* it.

A certain amount of anxiety may even be useful. It can provide the motivation to keep you on your toes during the test. Likewise, confidence is fine—but arrogance can be devastating. Your assessment of your abilities and preparation must bear some resemblance to reality.

Successful students have a plan

Tests are opportunities for you to shine and show your stuff. Many students, unfortunately, think studying for a test means looking at their notes the night before the exam. Effective test preparation requires continual review and practice.

So, how will you prepare for an exam? When? What study material will you use? What items will you need for test day? As the "big day" approaches, successful students establish a plan. Use the checklist in Activity 9.2 to get organized, reduce your levels of anxiety, and do well on your latest opportunity.

ACTIVITY 9.2   TEST PREPARATION CHECKLIST

Class: _____   Instructor: _____   Test date and time: _____

Type of exam:

- ○ Multiple choice
- ○ True/false
- ○ Matching
- ○ Completion
- ○ Identification
- ○ Essay
- ○ Lab work
- ○ Problems
- ○ Other _____

What do I need when I study?

- ○ Textbook
- ○ Notes
- ○ Teacher's study guide
- ○ Worksheets
- ○ Past exams (these can be very helpful!)
- ○ Supplemental readings
- ○ Calculator
- ○ Pens, pencils, paper
- ○ Other _____

Will I study alone or with a study group?   ○ Alone   ○ Study group
(A word of caution about study groups: make sure they are more study than social! Set an agenda.)

Are there any study sessions the teacher will lead before or after class?

○ Yes   ○ No

If "yes," when? _____

When will I study? Make a plan—and stick to it!

Date/time: _____

Date/time: _____

Date/time: _____

(Put these dates on your calendar.)

Prioritization. What topics will the exam cover?

Topic	I really know this stuff	I am not too sure about this stuff	I have no clue about this stuff!	Topic reviewed at least once
1.				
2.				
3.				
4.				

Predict some test questions. (This forces you to focus on the key concepts the teacher has been stressing.)

_____

_____

_____

_____

_____

_____

_____

_____

_____

_____

_____

What do I need for test day?
- ○ Pens, pencils, paper (lined, unlined, graph, bluebook)
- ○ Calculator
- ○ Notes—can I use my notes during the test?
- ○ Textbook—is the test open-book?
- ○ Ruler
- ○ Wristwatch
- ○ Tissue for sniffles
- ○ Other _____

(continued)

ACTIVITY 9.2 TEST PREPARATION CHECKLIST, continued

Test preparation does *not* end when you hand in your test. Start preparing for your next exam by doing a postexam analysis.

I was most prepared for _____

I was not well prepared for _____

Why? _____

The biggest help was:
- ○ My notes
- ○ My homework
- ○ Tutoring sessions
- ○ My study schedule
- ○ My study group
- ○ My study environment
- ○ Other _____

My major weakness(es) was:
- ○ Ran out of time during the test
- ○ Did not expect this type of test
- ○ Studied the wrong material
- ○ Did not start studying early enough
- ○ Other _____

Grade I *realistically* expect to receive _____   Grade I received _____

My *realistic* plan to improve for the next exam is

_____

_____

_____

_____

_____

_____

_____

_____

_____

_____

Postexam analysis

A common reaction by many students following the completion of an exam is to forget it and concentrate on the next opportunity. Although this is an understandable reaction, the successful student needs to pause, even if momentarily, and reflect on the exam.

Look at the checklist in Activity 9.2 once again. Notice that the last portion is a postexam analysis. This type of activity accomplishes a couple of things. While the material is still fresh in your mind, content review is critical. There is a good chance you will see some of this information again on a midterm or final examination. Make sure you have it correct now. Don't get it wrong again! From a process point of view, it is important to understand what did and did not work for you. Why not use this time to identify your challenges and strengths? Set a goal for the next exam.

Hey, isn't this where we started?
Assessment of strengths and weaknesses

Look back at Module 1. One of the first activities was an assessment of your strengths and weaknesses. Are you seeing a pattern here?

All of these strategies are a continual process. By reviewing, relating, and reorganizing (the 3Rs), you are able to move forward. The postexam analysis places you back at the goal-setting stage. Now, you are ready to improve your performance, establish a goal, evaluate, and improve again. That's really all there is to it.

Emergency studying

"Okay," you say. "Organization is great, but what do I do if I have not kept up? What do I do to survive a test when I'm down to the night before, and I'm not ready?" Here are some pointers for emergency studying. Please remember that this is not desirable, but if it's all you have, then let's get the most from it.

DO *NOT* . . .

- Be tempted to read quickly everything you have not read yet. If you read large quantities of knowledge too fast, you will have poor recall. Why waste your time?
- Panic! Okay, so you didn't study as you wish you had. Test day is no time to panic.
- Give up—especially on essay exams. Never leave the item blank. Think! You surely can come up with something to write. You just may get credit.

DO . . .

- Accept the fact you will not be able to study everything.
- Relax as best you can.
- Start by anticipating your teacher. What type of questions will the teacher ask? What types of content and/or skills will be tested? Recall? Relationships? (This will be much easier if you have been practicing the 3Rs.)
- Go to your notes and text to find the most important material. Clues to guide you: chapter titles and subtitles, major emphasis in class discussions and lectures, relationships with past material, chapter summaries. (Refer to the reading plan in Module 6.) Is a study group available?

- Follow these steps when you find important information:
  - Read it.
  - Ask yourself a question for which the information is an answer.
  - Say the information to yourself.
  - Check to see if you were correct.
  - Do it until you get it correct twice.
- Try to find and study some important information from every chapter that was assigned.

Next time, plan ahead and establish a study schedule.

Test-taking strategies

SUCCESS STRATEGY

GENERAL

- Get a good night's sleep prior to the exam. Do not study right up until bedtime. Give your brain a rest and do something nonacademic before going to bed. Otherwise, you might wake up feeling like you have not had a break. You want to be as sharp as possible going into the test.
- Depending on the time of the exam, eat a good breakfast or lunch, but don't overeat—this might leave you groggy. If you don't ordinarily eat breakfast or lunch, and that works for you, by all means don't eat. Use strategies that fit your lifestyle, body requirements, and personality.
- Have all your tools with you (see Activity 9.2).
- Wear a watch or, at the very least, have the class clock in your sight. It is your responsibility to keep track of time, not the teacher's. Be aware, though, that those school-issued room clocks are notorious for being slow, fast, or broken.
- Read *all* instructions carefully. Do *not* start until you know what you are expected to do. There really is no prize for finishing first!
- Know your material. Don't just memorize it. More than likely, the wording on the exam will be different from what you found in your book, or what the teacher said in class. Relate to the *Big Picture*. Review the strategies in Module 3 and the first topic of this module.

MULTIPLE-CHOICE TESTS

- Read carefully. Look for words such as *not, except, which is incorrect, best, all, always, never, none*.
- Block all the answer choices before you look at them. Treat the item like a fill-in-the-blank question. Come up with an answer before you look at the choices. This might keep you from being swayed by a "trick" answer.
- If you are not sure of an answer, use the process of elimination to arrive at the correct answer. At least you can narrow your options and make an educated guess.
- Answer the easy questions first; save the tough ones for the end.
- <u>Underline</u> key words.
- If you are using an answer sheet, make sure you transfer your answers to the correct number on the sheet.

MATCHING TESTS

- Read all the answer choices first.
- Cross out the items you pick. (Some instructors will not allow you to write on the exam. If this is the case for an exam you are taking, then make cross-out marks lightly with your pencil so that you can erase them before you turn in your exam.)
- Find out if you are allowed to use an answer more than once.
- Answer the easy items first; save the tough ones for the end.

ESSAY TESTS (REVIEW MODULE 7)

- Know what your task is. Once again, know these key words:

  analyze: to divide a topic or issue into its parts; to show the relation of one part to another

  apply: to use your knowledge in a new or different situation

  assess: to judge the merits of some issue; to evaluate

  classify: to put things into categories

  compare: to provide similarities, differences, consequences (see *analyze*)

  contrast: to provide differences

  criticize: to judge critically

  defend: to argue for a particular issue

  describe: to explain an event, issue, topic; to explain the main characteristics

  discuss: to explain in detail; to go beyond mere description

  evaluate: to judge, criticize, establish standards

  identify: to show how something is unique or individual

  illustrate: to provide examples

  interpret: to describe the meaning of an issue

  motivations: what caused something to happen

  relative importance: how two or more factors compare with one another

  summarize: to restate briefly

  trace: to provide an order or sequence of events

- Know what the essay topic is.
- Develop a main idea and follow it.
- Support your thesis with substantial facts; don't insult the teacher with "fluff."
- Pay attention to grammar and sentence structure.
- Never leave an essay item blank. Put something down—you might get credit.
- Don't forget to use the clustering strategy.
- If you tend to get writer's block, practice the strategies introduced in Module 7.

As you prepare for the exam, be kind to yourself. Don't sit there saying you are going to fail. Establish a goal and go for it. Successful students carry a positive attitude in their book bag.

Case Study 6

Test Preparation

APPLYING YOUR NEW SKILLS TO THE WORKPLACE

For this case study, you are given only the situation. You will supply a solution.

SITUATION. Veronica has been a nurse for 10 years at City Hospital. She is competent and always receives top evaluations. Her latest assignment placed her in the oncology unit. Here, she deals with mostly terminally ill cancer patients. Though it is a highly stressful and emotional job, Veronica believes she has found her career passion. This is where she wants to be.

"I feel I am bringing some relief and peace to my patients," Veronica recently tells a friend. "Some survive, many do not. But they all need quality care."

Veronica has always kept up with the latest research in her field. Now, at the urging of her head nurse, she has decided to take the national certification exam to add to her credentials. She must take the exam in two months—and now she's having second thoughts.

"I haven't taken an exam since I got my A.S. degree from City Community College," she tells her supervisor. "I don't think this is a good idea. Maybe I should just forget about it. The more I think about it, the more anxious I become. What if I fail? Won't that look just grand?"

Veronica's supervisor assures her that she will do fine. The test is difficult, but other coworkers have passed it. And even if she doesn't pass the exam, it won't affect her job status. She will still have her position.

Veronica sits at the kitchen table one evening after dinner. The study materials scattered before her look more and more ominous. There are eight major topics to study and a 600-page book to read. Some of the material she already knows from her day-to-day activities. Some she is only slightly knowledgeable about. And some she has never heard of.

"I'll never learn this stuff!" she says out loud as she puts her head in her hands and gently tugs at her hair in despair.

YOUR REACTION AND PROPOSED SOLUTION. Why do you think Veronica is having this difficulty? Is it possible for her to utilize some of the techniques you have learned in your class on test preparation? Using the SAC-SIP method of problem solving, help Veronica devise a plan.

Stop.

_____

_____

_____

Alternatives.

_____

_____

_____

Consequences.

_____

_____

_____

Selection.

_____

_____

_____

Implementation.

_____

_____

_____

Pause.

_____

_____

_____

YOUR REACTION.   Why do you believe the plan you propose is the best for Veronica? What potential problems exist with this solution?

A QUICK REVIEW

Effective test preparation starts at the completion of the most recent exam. This does not mean continual round-the-clock studying. In fact, if you follow the methods in these modules, your study time should be reduced. But for this to become a reality, you must

- see all the module topics as part of an interconnected whole; do not view them simply as separate and unrelated items.
- know if, and why, you are anxious about exams.
- be an efficient test taker.
- be familiar with your instructors' testing styles.
- start preparing for the next exam right after completing the most recent exam.
- always take a moment to do a postexam analysis.

Focus on success—not excuses!

Take a few minutes now to review Exhibits 9.2 and 9.3.

exhibit 9.2 Some possible correlations with your learning style.

TOPIC	AUDITORY	KINESTHETIC	VISUAL
Preparing for the exam	Utilize the 3Rs; tape-record potential exam questions.	Write questions on flash cards.	Write potential exam questions.
During the exam	Preview the entire exam; methodically work through items simplest to more difficult; if appropriate (and not distracting to others), say items aloud.	Preview the entire exam; physically block out all but the item you are working on.	Preview the entire exam; mark up the exam as much as is helpful.

exhibit 9.3 How to complement selected intelligences.

WHEN GIVEN AN ASSIGNMENT OR TASK, IF YOU ARE STRONG IN . . .	THEN ASK YOURSELF . . .
Interpersonal intelligence/ tutoring	"How can I use this intelligence to make the most out of a tutoring opportunity?"
Intrapersonal intelligence/ study group	"How can I use my self-knowledge to determine if a study group is best for me?"
Linguistic intelligence/review	"How can I use this ability to review my exam material?"

Here are some things you can do to improve your learning environment:

- Determine whether a study group is appropriate for you.
- Set up a schedule of studying to coincide with your "peak times."
- Limit distracting stimuli.
- Practice good nutritional and sleep habits in order to enhance test performance.

Complete the following exercises.

1. Evaluate the opening quote by Roberts.

   _____

   _____

   _____

2. List three of the test-anxiety categories presented in Activity 9.1, and give two examples of each.

   A. _____

   B. _____

   C. _____

3. Describe three strategies you can use to address test anxiety.

   A. _____

   B. _____

   C. _____

4. Why is the postexam analysis an important step?

   _____

   _____

   _____

   _____

Checklist

Checklist of Selected Tips and Strategies

As a last review, collaborate with a classmate and write a brief description of how each of the following will help you become a more successful student.

TEST PREPARATION

1. Understanding that test preparation is essential

2. Recognizing and solving test anxiety

3. Being kind to yourself

4. Enhancing test-taking efficiency

5. Visualizing success

6. Having confidence without arrogance

7. Utilizing the checklist

8. Utilizing postexam analysis—establishing a modified goal

9. Doing emergency studying

10. Getting adequate sleep

11. Eating properly

12. Having your tools

13. Wearing your watch

14. Carefully reading instructions

15. Looking for key words

SUCCESS
STRATEGY

A 14-STEP GUIDE TO BETTER STUDY HABITS

1. Make a commitment. "I want to be a more successful student!" Say it out loud.

2. Establish a realistic goal, based on your learning style, concerning your study habits. Set a target date. Make your plan to reach that goal.

3. Write down the steps to reaching your goal and place it where you will see it each day.

4. Make sure you have a quiet area with an appropriate study area environment for your learning style.

5. Get a calendar—and use it.

6. Find a buddy and an academic coach. Besides you and your teachers, these two people will be your most important resources.

7. Keep a time log for at least one week. How do you spend your time? How do you want to spend your time?

8. Schedule quality study time—and use it. It's okay to be flexible, but don't neglect this step.

9. Make sure you understand the major points of each module. Get nine pieces of notebook paper. In the middle of each page, write the main topic of each module. Develop a scattergram of the chapter contents (see Module 5). Write the main points and specific strategies. When you have completed reading the module, develop a thesis statement that adequately summarizes the main topic. Do this for all modules.

10. Concentrate. When distractions strike, quickly acknowledge them and then move on to your studies.

11. Develop active learning skills. Use as much of your brain as possible.

12. Leave time for recreation. Remember to keep a balance in your life. School is your "job," but don't become fanatical.

13. When overwhelmed with schoolwork, remember to simplify.

14. Continually reevaluate your goals. Change direction if necessary. This does not mean bail out at the first sign of an obstacle. Be flexible, and take a step toward your goal each day.

IN CLOSING

You lead a busy life! No one knows that better than you. I want to congratulate you on your desire and commitment to improve your academic performance. Many students are left wondering what the connection is between the classroom and the real world. You have now bridged that gap. Success sometimes is accompanied by setback. Keep your eye on your goals and steadily move toward them. Best wishes for a proud and satisfying future.

"To climb steep hills requires slow pace at first."

—WILLIAM SHAKESPEARE

SELECTED BIBLIOGRAPHY

Further reading and research will foster success. You may find the following sources especially helpful.

Armstrong, Thomas. *Multiple Intelligences in the Classroom.* Alexandria, VA: Association for Supervision and Curriculum Development, 1994.

Bender, Sheila. *Writing Personal Essays: How to Shape Your Life Experiences for the Page.* Cincinnati, OH: Writer's Digest Books, 1995.

Canter, Lee, and Lee Hausner. *Homework Without Tears.* New York: HarperPerennial, 1987.

Carter, Carol, Joyce Bishop, and Sarah L. Kravits. *Keys to Success: How to Achieve Your Goals.* 4th ed. Upper Saddle River, NJ: Prentice Hall, 2003.

Coman, Marcia, and Kathy Heavers. *How to Improve Your Study Skills.* Chicago: VGM Career Horizons/NTC Publishing Group, 1990.

Covey, Stephen R. *The 7 Habits of Highly Effective People.* New York: Simon & Schuster, 1989. Audiocassette.

Covey, Stephen R., A. Roger Merrill, and Rebecca R. Merrill. *First Things First.* New York: Simon & Schuster, 1994.

Disney University Professional Development Programs. *Creating Motivational Learning Environments.* Orlando, FL: Walt Disney World Company, 1995.

Dunn, Rita, and Kenneth Dunn. *Teaching Students Through Their Individual Learning Styles: A Practical Approach.* Reston, VA: Reston Publishing, 1978.

Ellis, Dave. *Becoming a Master Student.* 7th ed. Boston: Houghton Mifflin, 1994.

Florey, Henry E., Jr. *Study Orientation Skills: Participant Manual.* Tuscaloosa, AL: Author, 1987.

Fry, Ron. *How To Study.* Hawthorne, NJ: The Career Press, 1991. [This series includes various titles: *Manage Your Time; Write Papers; Take Notes; Improve Your Reading; Ace Any Test; Improve Your Memory.*]

Gardner, Howard. *Frames of Mind: The Theory of Multiple Intelligences.* New York: Basic Books, 1993.

Gilbert, Sarah. *Go for It: Get Organized.* New York: Morrow Jr. Books, 1990.

Green, Gordon W., Jr. *Helping Your Child Learn.* New York: Carol Publishing Group, 1994.

Keefe, James. *Learning Style Profile Handbook: Accommodating Perceptual, Study and Instructional Preferences (Vol. II).* Reston, VA: National Association of Secondary School Principals, 1989.

Koepple, Mary Sue. *Writing Resources for Conferencing and Collaboration.* Upper Saddle River, NJ: Prentice Hall, 1989.

Lazear, David. *Seven Ways of Knowing: Teaching for Multiple Intelligences.* Palatine, IL: Skylight, 1991.

Margulies, Nancy. *Mapping Inner Space: Learning and Teaching Mind Mapping.* Tucson, AA: Zephyr Press, 1991.

Matte, Nancy L., and Susan H. G. Henderson. *Success Your Style! Right- and Left-Brain Techniques for Learning.* Belmont, CA: Wadsworth, 1995.

Minninger, Joan, and Eleanor Dugan. *Rapid Memory in 7 Days: The Quick-and-Easy Guide to Better Remembering.* New York: Perigee, 1994.

Noble, William. *The 28 Biggest Writing Blunders: And How to Avoid Them.* Cincinnati, OH: Writer's Digest Books, 1992.

Olney, Claude W. *Where There's a Will There's an "A".* Paoli, PA: Chesterbrook Educational Publishers, 1990. Videocassette.

Pauk, Walter. *How to Study in College.* 5th ed. Boston: Houghton Mifflin, 1993.

Piscitelli, Steve. *Does Anyone Understand This Stuff? A Student Guide to Organizing United States History.* Atlantic Beach, FL: Author, 2001.

Robinson, Adam. *What Smart Students Know: Maximum Grades, Optimum Learning, Minimum Time.* New York: Crown Trade Paperbacks, 1993.

Scharf-Hunt, Diana, and Pam Hait. *Studying Smart: Time Management for College Students.* New York: HarperPerennial, 1990.

Silver, Theodore. *Study Smart: Hands-on, Nuts-and-Bolts Techniques for Earning Higher Grades.* New York: Villard Books, 1992.

Swartz, Roger G. *Accelerated Learning: How You Learn Determines What You Learn.* Durant, OK: EMIS, 1991.

Trudeau, Kevin. *Mega Memory.* Niles, IL: Nightingale Conant, 1991. Audiocassette.

Wahlstrom, Carl, and Brian K. Williams. *Learning Success: Three Paths to Being Your Best at College Life.* Belmont, CA: Wadsworth, 1999.

Wilson, Susan B. *Goal Setting.* New York: American Management Association, 1994.

Winstead, Elizabeth. "Mastering Time Management." Jacksonville, FL: Jacksonville University, no date. A seminar presentation.

Ziglar, Zig. *How to Get What You Want.* New York: Simon & Schuster, 1978. Audiocassette.

INDEX